50 great curries
of thailand
vatcharin bhumichitr

Vatcharin Bhumichitr was born and educated in Bangkok. He moved to London in 1976 and later started a business importing Thai food and ingredients, before opening his first restaurant in 1980 and going on to become one of the UK's premier Thai chefs and restaurateurs. His previous books include *The Big Book of Thai Curries*, *The Big Book of Noodles* and *Stylish Thai in Minutes*. His latest projects include resorts in Ko Samui and Chiang Mail, where he offers cooking courses and art classes – in addition to his success as a chef, Vatch is a talented artist. To find out more about Vatch, or to contact him, visit www.vatchthailand.com.

50 great curries of thailand
vatcharin bhumichitr

photography by Martin Brigdale &

Somchai Phongphaisarnkit

kyle books

This edition published in Great Britain in 2015 by
Kyle Books, an imprint of Kyle Cathie Ltd
192–198 Vauxhall Bridge Road
London SW1V 1DX
general.enquiries@kylebooks.com
www.kylebooks.com

Printer line 10 9 8 7 6 5 4 3

ISBN 978 0 85783 290 0

Text © 2004, 2007, 2010, 2015 Vatcharin Bhumichitr*
Design © 2015 Kyle Books
Food photography © 2007, 2015 Martin Brigdale**
Location photography © 2007, 2015 Somchai Phongphaisarnkit***
*Recipes on pages 169, 172 and 184–185 originally published in *The Big Book of Noodles*;
recipes on pages 170, 171, 177, 178, 180, and 183 originally published in *Stylish Thai in
Minutes*; all other recipes originally published in *The Big Book of Thai Curries*
**except pages 168 & 173, © Will Heap
*** except pages 6–7, 30–31, 50–51, 52–53, 138–139, 162–163, 174–175 © istock photo/
enviromantic; pages 68–69 © istock photo/Rolf_52; pages 92–93 © istock photo/Michael
Luhrenberg; pages 114–115 © istock photo/KHellon; page 176 © istock photo/varandah

Project Editor: Tara O'Sullivan
Design: Tara O'Sullivan
Series Design: Geoff Hayes
Photographers: Martin Brigdale and Somchai Phongphaisarnkit
Food Stylists: Annie Rigg and Linda Tubby
Prop Stylist: Helen Trent
Production: Nic Jones, Gemma John and Lisa Pinnell

A Cataloguing in Publication record for this title is available from the
British Library.

Colour reproduction by ALTA London
Printed and bound in China by C&C Offset Printing Co., Ltd.

contents

'kin khao lua lang!'

This is the traditional greeting you will hear all over Thailand. Unlike Western greetings, it doesn't mean 'how are you?' or 'hello'. It means 'have you eaten yet?'. This shows just how central food is to the Thai way of life. If the reply is no, the greeting will often be followed by an invitation to eat. And for a group of Thais sitting down to a meal, the first question is invariably *'kin gaeng arai dee?'* or 'what curry shall we eat?'. The type of curry (green, red, yellow, etc.) and the kind of meat or fish to go in it are discussed first. Only when this is decided will the conversation turn to other elements of the meal – the stir-fries or steamed dishes and their respective ingredients.

servings and quantities

The recipes in this book are for four to six people, and they tell you how to make curries as authentic as those you would find in Thailand. When you start making the curries I hope you will experiment, adjusting the quantities of the ingredients to create a hotter, milder, sweeter or more sour taste – just as cooks do in Thailand – so you develop the flavours that you prefer. The best way to learn about Thai curries is to make a big pot, invite your friends over, have a party and enjoy yourself.

what is thai cooking?

Originally, Thai people lived a waterborne lifestyle, mainly in the central plains of Thailand, travelling on and living by the rivers, growing rice and catching fish, which was cooked on a wood-fire grill or barbecue. To accompany the fish, they developed dips and sauces, which were made from locally grown herbs, spices, peppers, cucumbers, aubergines and other vegetables, some of which were grown in the rivers, along with various types of limes and lemongrass. The vegetables were, and still are, often eaten raw. As this diet is somewhat dry, soups developed, such as the well-known tom yam, which was originally made with fish. At that time, the Thais shunned eating large animals, and when meat was eaten it was always chopped into small pieces. This is thought to be because of their Buddhist heritage.

During the sixteenth century, foreigners started to appear in Thailand, introducing significant new ingredients, such as the chilli. Since that time, the Thais have adopted many foreign foods, including curries from India and Persia, and noodles from China, but they have always been adapted to suit the Thai way of eating, thereby producing a taste unique to Thailand. Food inevitably becomes individual to the place where it is being prepared and cooked, because the local ingredients always have a taste and texture different to anywhere else.

Nowadays, fruit and vegetables that are associated with certain parts of the world can be bought anywhere, and so, sadly, this individuality is gradually being lost. I am glad to say, though, that it still exists in Thailand.

Right: Seafood in a Thai market.

curries and thai cooking

I always feel lucky to have been born in Thailand. The country is very fertile, irrigated as it is by the great Chao Phraya and other rivers. Thailand is largely an agricultural society, growing rice, fruit and vegetables and raising animals. The Gulf of Thailand is teeming with fish, the climate is good and most foods grow very easily here. If you stay in the countryside, you quickly become aware that nearly all you need to survive grows around you.

In the villages, a strong culture of sharing resources was once common; one household would slaughter an animal and it would be shared among everyone in the village.

Rice farmers in Thailand are the backbone of Thai agriculture and their crop is the lifeblood of the country. Glutinous or 'sticky' rice is popular in the north and northeast, but in the rest of the country the long-grain variety is dominant. For many years, rice was the country's main export and it still remains the staple of the Thai diet, providing strength and energy.

To bulk up the rice and add flavour, a spicy, fairly runny, curry sauce is always served – the effect is to make you eat more rice! Traditionally, rice is eaten three times a day and curry can be eaten at any, or all, of these meals. As you would expect, the various regions of Thailand have developed their own specialities of curry by using their locally grown herbs and spices. The curries of the country's border regions also often reflect the cuisines of adjacent nations. There is a strong Laotian influence in the northeast, a Burmese influence in the north, Malay and Muslim influences in the south, and so on.

The culinary influence of different countries also goes beyond Thailand's immediate neighbours. Sri Lanka, India and Persia have all had their inputs, but now Thai curries have developed their own individual tastes, colours and textures.

My mother's speciality was green beef curry. In a big family like ours, she would cook a large pot of curry to feed us all. My father was always busy working or entertaining, but whenever he ate at home he would ask for green curry. I was the same; just before term ended when I was studying in London, I phoned home to ensure a curry would be ready when I arrived back in Bangkok.

One of my brothers even told his future wife that his one requirement was that she learned to cook green curry just like our mother!

Right: An array of red, green, pale green and yellow chillies. Bigger chillies tend to be milder and are often dried to intensify their flavour. Thai cucumbers can be seen on the far right of the picture.

what does curry mean?

The word 'curry' is a derivative of the Tamil word '*kari*'. This was used in India to describe a type of dish with a strong flavour and aroma caused by the herbs and spices used in the cooking. They were often used to disguise poor-quality meat, which in the old days could be pretty tough and 'high'. A few Thai curries do resemble the Indian version, in which case the name *kari* is used, but the more usual term in Thailand is *gaeng pet*. This literally means 'thickened spicy liquid'.

Gaeng pet has a broader application than the English word 'curry' and can be used to describe any savoury dish that has been thickened with a paste.

Curry paste was, and still is, prepared by pounding the ingredients individually in a mortar. If you walk around some residential areas in Thailand in the morning, you will hear the rhythmic pounding of pestles and mortars all around you. Each housewife produces her own characteristic beat as she grinds out the paste for that day's curry. Today, however, most people buy their curry pastes, either freshly made in the local market or prepacked from a supermarket.

Many of the ingredients in Thai curry pastes are considered healthy and even medicinal (garlic is an obvious example), but their texture or taste can make them difficult or unpleasant to eat alone. Pounding and mixing them together gets round this problem, and, when the flavours are skilfully blended, ingredients that might be unpalatable on their own become part of something delicious.

Right: Different ready-made curry pastes for sale.

Left: Stone mortar and pestles last for years and are handed down through the generations. It always amazes me that there is still a market for them!

the differences between a Thai and an Indian curry

The most obvious difference between Thai and Indian curries is that Thai curries are cooked with herbs and spices that are nearly always fresh, whereas Indian curries use dried ones. And while Indian curries are usually based on ghee or yogurt, Thais typically use coconut milk. The resulting textures are as subtly contrasting as cow's milk and soya milk. Another difference is that Thai curries combine vegetables with meat or fish, while in India the vegetables are often served as separate dishes.

what's special about thai curries?

Because they are based on fresh ingredients, Thai curries are uniquely light and refreshing. They also have very distinctive colours. These are determined by the colour of their ingredients, mostly the chillies and the curry pastes, hence the famous red, green and yellow varieties.

where does the heat in thai curries come from?

The heat in Thai curries comes from chillies, pepper (both white and black), garlic, galangal, coriander and onion. All these ingredients are hot in varying degrees. But while heat is a feature of many of the curries in this book, it should always be balanced by three other key tastes in Thai cuisine: sweet, sour and salty. Sweetness is provided by ingredients such as sugar and Thai basil; sourness by tamarind and lime; and saltiness by fish sauce.

Left: Chillies are an essential part of the flavour combinations found in Thai curries.

the role of curry in a thai meal

When we discuss what to eat, we first choose a type of curry (red, green, orange, jungle) and the main ingredient (beef, pork, fish, etc.). At home, after we finish dinner, we discuss what we are going to eat the following day. Once we have decided on the curry and its ingredients, we then decide on the accompanying vegetables, taking into account what is in season and so on. These will be cooked in a stir-fry. We may then choose another dish to balance the other flavours. If the curry is pork, for example, the third dish might be fish fried with garlic and chilli. We also select a dessert. Early in the morning, someone will go out to the market and buy all the fresh ingredients for the evening meal. In the afternoon, we prepare the curry and the dessert, which takes about thirty minutes. The remaining dishes are cooked around 7pm and ready on the table for dinner an hour later.

curry is eaten all day

When I was at school, much like today, there was food for sale at lunchtime, or you could take your own lunchbox. I usually had some toast and hot chocolate, or eggs and bacon for breakfast. For lunch, I would eat curry noodles, and in the evening we would have a meal based around a curry. In many households, particularly in the countryside, they will cook a large pot of curry early in the morning, which will be eaten throughout the day by the whole family. The children will take it to eat at school and the adults will take it out to the fields where they go to work. In the evening, it will form the basis of the meal, to be eaten together with a stir-fry and a soup.

When you travel on the motorways of Thailand, as in other countries, there are service stations, which generally have a small selection of food outlets. In Thailand, these are normally run by local people. There will be a wide selection of precooked food, several different curries and stir-fried dishes, omelettes and fried eggs. You are given a plate of boiled rice, and then you pick a spoonful or two of different dishes to be placed on top of the rice. You can choose as many as you wish, although any more than three or four toppings and the flavours can become a little confused. This will normally be eaten with a selection of raw vegetables, which, along with the condiments, will be provided for you at the table.

the composition of thai curry

why is the combination of coriander, lemongrass and garlic so thai?

There are three main reasons why the combination of coriander, lemongrass and garlic is so typical of Thai cooking. The first has to do with convenience. All these ingredients grow quickly and abundantly throughout Thailand and they are available all year round. Most urban households will have them growing in the garden. Lemongrass grows just like regular grass, only with more of a tendency to form clumps. Garlic and coriander are also fast growing, and the latter has the advantage of furnishing the cook with three distinct products: seeds, roots and leaves.

The second reason for the importance of these ingredients in Thai cuisine is their contribution to a healthy diet. Unlike Westerners, Thais do not make a clear distinction between food and medicine, and all three plants are considered medicinal. Coriander is believed to enhance the appetite, improve digestion and clear phlegm. Lemongrass is another appetite stimulant and considered to be good for headaches and fevers. Garlic, meanwhile, is thought to cleanse the blood.

Unsurprisingly, the final reason why coriander, lemongrass and garlic are so central in Thai cooking is all about taste. All three contribute to the perfumed clarity that is so characteristic of Thai dishes, both individually and together.

Coriander, as mentioned above, yields three distinct ingredients. The fibrous roots are used as a flavourful binding agent in curry pastes. The seeds are ground to produce a spice with an orange aroma, and the leaves provide pungency as well as an attractive garnish.

Lemongrass lends a fresh citrus taste with hints of mint and ginger. It cuts through oils and fats, giving zest to dishes that would otherwise be cloying on the palate.

Garlic is used to flavour cooking oils (Thais don't like to use oils with a strong flavour of their own) and to provide an aromatic, but largely hidden, base for savoury dishes.

Any Thai cook will have learned through experience the skill of balancing the flavours of coriander, lemongrass and garlic according to their own preference. As a result, the cumulative taste will vary from cook to cook and area to area. There is no such thing as the correct combination, only a personal one, which is developed over a lifetime of cooking with these three key ingredients.

Left: Anticlockwise from bottom – lemongrass, kaffir lime leaves, galangal, mint, kaffir limes, krachai

other key ingredients in thai curries

chillies

These were introduced into Thailand around four hundred years ago by Portuguese traders who imported them from South America. Prior to this, the heat element in Thai food came from pepper and galangal. There are several kinds of chilli used in Thailand. Here I will introduce you to the five key varieties.

The hottest is the *prik kee noo suan*, which translates as 'mouse droppings' (the similarity is in the shape!). *Prik kee noo suan* chillies are green when young and ripen to red. When red, the taste is hotter, but the chillies have no aroma. When green they are milder (although still very hot for Western tastes), but have a noticeable aroma.

Next on the hotness scale is *prik kee noo* (without the suan), which is called the birdseye chilli in the West. It is at least 2.5cm long and slightly less hot than the 'mouse dropping', but still pretty fierce.

The third is called *prik chee faa*. It can be either red or green and is about 7.5–10cm in length. *Prik chee faa* are slightly less hot than the smaller varieties, but should still be handled with caution.

Prik haeng are large sun-dried red chillies similar in size to *prik chee faa*. They are deep maroon/red and need to be soaked, cut into pieces, then allowed to dry again before use.

The final chilli is the *prik yuak*. It is large, pale yellow-green and shaped rather like the sweet bell peppers eaten in the West. If a recipe calls for *prik yuak* and you don't have any available, you can use a white Hungarian paprika chilli or even a regular sweet pepper instead.

Thais believe that if you burn a chilli covered in salt it will remove any 'bad spirits' that may be around you. The Isaan people from northeast Thailand believe that eating very hot chillies will strengthen you, and the hotter you can eat the more 'manly' you are.

Left: The whole coriander plant is used and sold in big bunches. Right: Prik kee noo *chillies*

sweet basil and holy basil

Several varieties of basil grow in Thailand, but sweet basil and holy basil are the ones familiar in the West because they travel well. Sweet basil is an annual herbaceous plant, the fresh leaves of which are either eaten raw or used as a flavouring in Thai cooking. It is not unlike the basil used in the Mediterranean. Thai or holy Basil has narrower leaves and is sometimes tinged with a reddish-purple colour. It has a stronger taste than sweet basil, which is only released when cooked.

shrimp paste

Kapee or shrimp paste is a pungent preserve used extensively in Thai cooking. It is made by pounding shrimp with salt and leaving them to decompose. *Kapee* smells fairly unpleasant when it is raw (some Thai farmers use it to keep monkeys off their crops!), but, as soon as you cook it, the overwhelming odour disappears. I often think that the smell has the same effect on an untrained nose as walking into a cheese shop does for a Thai person! *Kapee* is at the heart of many curry pastes, and can be used to flavour boiled rice. Mixed with other ingredients, such as garlic, chilli, fish sauce and lemon juice, it makes *nam prik*, a hot runny paste that is served with fried fish or as a dip for raw vegetables.

Above left: Sweet basil
Right: Selling kapee (shrimp paste). The price is per kilo (in Thai baht) and ranges from a cheap version made with offcuts of fish, to the most expensive version, which is made with good-quality shrimp.

regional differences

Like most cuisines, Thai food is very local. Dishes developed in specific regions because the people were using what grew around them there. The cuisine has developed on that basis.

Thailand can be divided into four geographical regions, each of which has its own culinary characteristics. The central plains, in which Bangkok is situated, are the most fertile part of the country and the most typically 'Thai'. Because communications are good and the region is the centre of business and government, the central plains have absorbed cooking practices from all over the country. As a result, all the classic Thai curries are eaten in the area. They tend to lie somewhere in the middle on the hotness scale.

Northern Thailand consists of a series of upland valleys and is ethnically diverse, with hill tribes and a noticeable Burmese influence. The climate is too cool for coconut palms, so coconut oil is not a feature of local curries. The traditional frying medium used to be rendered pork fat, which gave northern food a special silky richness, but nowadays most people use vegetable oil. Curries from this fertile region are typically less hot than in the rest of the country. One possible reason for this is that ingredients were historically so plentiful in the area that there was no need to make very spicy food to make a little go a long way.

The northeast of Thailand is known as Isaan. It consists of a plateau about 300 metres above sea level and was very isolated and forested until the nineteenth century. The northeast has an extreme climate, with a long, dry season followed by frequent floods. The fertility of the soil in the region is not good, which may be why, in contrast to the north, its curries are often extremely hot. Food was often scarce and the spicier it was, the further it would go. Other features of northeastern cuisine include the use of glutinous, rather than long-grain, rice, small dried red chillies and a fondness for fermented fish (*plaa raa*) as a seasoning.

Coconut palms grow all over in southern Thailand, so coconut cream and milk feature strongly in local curries. Fishing is the most important part of the economy and seafood is abundant. This part of the country was the first point of contact with traders from India and Arabia, so many of its curries show their influence, for instance in the use of turmeric. This is also the most Islamic part of Thailand – about a third of the population is Muslim – and there is a sharp distinction between the curries made by Muslims and Buddhists in the region. The former are usually cooked with ghee (clarified butter) or yogurt plus stock, whereas Buddhists use coconut cream. Curries in the south are quite hot and tend to incorporate yellow chillies and fiery birdseye chillies, rather than the long red ones used further north. The cooking of the far south also has a strong Malay influence.

what is the difference between wet and dry curries?

Some Thai curries use quite a lot of liquid, which can be coconut milk, stock or water, and so have a soupy or stew-like consistency. Therefore, they are sometimes called wet curries. The idea is that the sauce will coat and cling to the rice served with them. Dry curries, such as Spicy Pork with Long Beans on page 101 and Hot Dry Beef Curry on page 107, have little or no liquid added after the paste has been fried.

Above: Produce in a Thai market.
Left: Floating street food in Bangkok. The calls of 'Curry noodles coming now!' entice people to come to the canal side to eat.

making a thai curry

how do I structure a curry?

Most of the curries in this book are fried. This means that during the first stage, the relevant curry paste is gently fried in oil. This is usually vegetable oil, but some of the recipes call for the paste to be fried in the oily component of coconut cream (for example, the Chicken Curry with Sour Bamboo Shoots on page 80). This entails first heating the coconut cream over a low heat until the solids and oil start to separate and will ensure that the paste fries properly. If the coconut cream hasn't separated, it will boil instead, which will not produce the desired taste. In Thailand, coconut cream is usually freshly made, so this is not a problem. The trouble with prepacked coconut cream is that it is often homogenised, which prevents it from separating properly. Try to buy non-homogenised coconut creams and milks. There are various brands available and the labels will give you the necessary information. If a recipe calls for the curry paste to be fried in coconut cream and you only have the homogenised kind, add a little vegetable oil to ensure the paste genuinely fries.

If you are making a fried curry, the second stage is usually to add the main ingredient (meat, fish or vegetables) and fry for a few minutes. The third stage is to add the liquid, which will be coconut milk, stock or water, depending on the recipe. It is important that you follow the correct sequence if you want your curries to taste authentic.

The other kind of curry popular in Thailand, particularly in the north, is boiled rather than fried. This involves dissolving the curry paste in the cooking liquid rather than in oil. A good example is Haddock with Green Curry Sauce on page 118.

Left: Green curry paste being prepared

what kind of oil should I use to fry the curry paste?

I recommend that you use peanut or sunflower oils, as they have very little taste of their own and therefore do not mask the delicate flavours of the other ingredients. Strong-tasting frying mediums, such as olive oil, should be avoided.

can you reheat a curry?

When curry is sold as street food in Thailand, cold curry is poured over hot rice, so warming up the sauce. In Thai homes, a big pot of curry is cooked in the morning and reheated for lunch and for the evening meal. At other times of the day it can be served with hot rice to warm it up.

what can you do to intensify the flavour of a curry?

Adding lemongrass or lime leaves to the stock used in the cooking of a curry will give it a stronger and more fragrant flavour. Another way to perk up a bland tasting curry is to use *nam pra prik*. To make enough to accompany one curry, combine 1 tablespoon fish sauce, the juice from ¼ lemon and 1 finely chopped small red chilli in a little bowl. Most homes have *nam pra prik* made up and ready to hand for those who prefer their curries to have a more intense taste.

Right: Kaffir lime leaves

curry paste ingredients

These are the core components of a Thai curry paste. These ingredients are used for stage 1 of cooking.

cardamom

A warm spice encased in green, black or creamy beige pods – green being the most common. Whole pods are used to flavour rice and meat dishes, particularly in the Muslim-influenced south. The pods themselves should not be eaten.

chillies

See page 21 for the common types of chillies.

cinnamon

Available as sticks or ground, cinnamon has a woody aroma with a warm, fragrant flavour. Cinnamon trees are native to Sri Lanka.

cloves

This sweet, warming spice is used in both savoury and sweet dishes, but like most dried spices, its use in Thai cooking is largely confined to Muslim dishes in the south.

coriander

This herb, the leaves of which are also known as Chinese parsley or cilantro, is widely featured in Thai dishes and as a garnish. Leaves, seeds, stems and the roots are all used. See page 19 for more.

Above: Coriander

galangal

Galangal is a rhizome plant that looks rather like ginger but has pink root tips and a unique, pungent flavour. In the West, ginger is often used to replace it, but the dishes won't taste the same.

garlic

Thai garlic cloves are small with thin, papery skin, which we often don't bother to peel away before use, but if you are using Western garlic you should peel it. See page 19 for more.

ginger

The root of this tuber should be peeled, then sliced, finely chopped or shredded. As with most herbs and foods, it tastes better fresh. Fresh ginger is known for its warm, pungent flavour. A native of southeast Asia, it is used in many intriguing spice combinations.

kaffir lime

This knobbly lime is roughly the same size and shape as the common lime, but has little juice. The peel is often used in recipes for curry pastes.

kaffir lime leaves

The dark green, glossy leaves of the kaffir lime impart a pungent lemon-lime flavour to dishes. They are available in some supermarkets and oriental stores. They keep well and can be frozen.

krachai (Chinese Key)

This annual plant has aromatic rhizomes and yellow brown roots, and is used as a flavouring. It also has a medicinal value as an aid to digestion.

lemongrass

Fresh lemongrass is common to many dishes throughout southeast Asia. Its rich lemon flavour combines well with other wet spices. Lemongrass is also available dried but tastes inferior. See page 19 for more.

nutmeg

Another spice used in some recipes from the south of Thailand, nutmeg comes in the form of dark brown or white 'nuts'. These should be kept whole in an airtight container and grated when needed. Ground nutmeg does not keep.

peppercorns

The white, green and black peppercorns are berries from the same plant, picked at different stages of maturity. They are used whole and ground.

Above: Kaffir lime

Above: Krachai (Chinese Key) – see page 33

shallots

The shallot is a member of the onion family, but it has a sweeter and milder taste. Thai shallots are so sweet that they are sometimes used in desserts! When buying shallots, go for the smaller ones. Larger specimens tend to be too oniony.

shrimp paste

This is a strongly flavoured paste used to flavour rice and curries. See page 22.

star anise

These are star-shaped, liquorice-flavoured pods indigenous to China. Like cardamom, the pods are used whole during cooking and should not be eaten.

tamarind

An acidic-tasting tropical fruit which resembles a bean pod. It gives a sharp flavour to curries. Tamarind is sold dried or pulped, and needs to be dissolved in hot water to extract the juice (see page 78).

turmeric

Another member of the ginger family, this can occasionally be found fresh in oriental stores, but more frequently in powdered form. When the whole spice is peeled or scraped, a rich golden root is revealed. Turmeric adds a distinctive flavour and rich yellow colour to dishes.

liquid ingredients

These ingredients are the liquid element of Thai curries and are usually added in stage 2 of cooking.

fish sauce (*nam pla*)

This is the basic savoury flavouring of Thai cooking, for which there is no substitute. Available bottled in oriental stores, it imparts a very distinctive salty flavour. It is made by pounding small fresh fish and/or shrimp with salt and leaving the mixture to ferment for a year or so. The resulting liquid is then strained and bottled. The best *nam pla* has a light whisky colour and a refreshing taste. Darker versions are often heavy and bitter – I tend to avoid them. Darkness in a fish sauce is also a sign that the bottle has been open too long. If your *nam pla* has changed colour significantly, you should replace it. Commercial fish sauces vary quite a lot in taste and saltiness, so experiment until you find a brand you like. You should also adjust the amount you use in a recipe according to its saltiness. Use taste as your guide. As ever, you are aiming to make sure the flavours are balanced.

soy sauce (*siew*)

Of the two types of soy sauce, the light version is thin, with a clear, delicate salty flavour and is the one most commonly used in cooking. Dark soy sauce adds colour as well as flavour to a dish. Use Thai, Malay or Vietnamese soy sauce for cooking; the Japanese version is too dark and has the wrong flavour.

bean sauce (*tow jiew*)

Tow jiew is a thickish sauce made from crushed, fermented and salted soya beans mixed with flour and spices. Varieties are made using both black and yellow beans, although the black bean kind is more common. *Tow jiew* is sold in jars or tins. Once opened, it should be kept in the fridge.

Right: Containers full of fermenting fish sauce with empty bottles ready to be filled. The fish sauce may be left for a year to 'cook' in the sun. The first pressing is used for cheaper brands of fish sauce, whereas the second pressing will be better quality and therefore more expensive.

Above: Fish sauce bottled and packaged for sale.
Right: Coconut waiting to be grated and
squeezed to make milk or cream.

stock

When a recipe calls for stock, the finished dish will be much better if you make it yourself rather than using shop-bought varieties. The way I make stocks is extremely simple. For a chicken, beef or pork stock, I place the bones in a large pan with no other ingredients, cover them with water and simmer for about 2 hours, skimming off any impurities as they rise to the surface. For a vegetable stock, I place 1 onion, 2 carrots and 2 celery stalks in a large pan of water, together with some coriander stalks and a few black peppercorns, and simmer them until the liquid has reduced by about a fifth, then strain.

coconut milk

For all these recipes, I have assumed you will use tinned coconut milk. If the recipe requires coconut cream, open the tin without shaking it and separate the thicker white cream from the transparent liquid, scooping it out with a ladle. Many people think that coconut milk is made from the watery juice inside the coconut. In fact, it is made by grating the white flesh, mixing it with warm water, then pressing it. The milk is used extensively in Thai curries and desserts. Dairy milk and products were completely unknown in Thailand until recently – they are not used in Thai cooking, except in the Muslim dishes of the south. Instead, Thais use coconut milk and coconut cream. Both are marketed worldwide in cartons, tins and blocks, and also now in powdered form. If you can find grated coconut (unsweetened, not the desiccated kind), you can also make coconut milk by mixing it with warm water and squeezing it. Making your own milk from the coconut flesh is hard work, but it does give a better flavour. It is worth trying if you want to make a really special curry.

making curry pastes

Above: Soaking dried chillies

For the true taste of a Thai curry, the paste needs to be freshly made, not bought. It is best done by pounding the ingredients using a stone pestle and mortar. In Thailand, a good pestle and mortar will be handed down from mother to daughter over several generations. In the old days, each ingredient was prepared individually before being pounded together to achieve the correct consistency. Dried red chillies, for example, have to be soaked, sliced into small pieces, then pounded with coarse salt to break down the chilli skin and achieve the correct texture. There is no doubt that, prepared this way, you get the freshest taste. It is an easy matter to alter the balance of flavours by adjusting the quantities of the different ingredients – more chilli, less pepper, etc.

However, preparing the paste in this way is time consuming and hard work. Until about 60 years ago, it was the only way to prepare curry paste and it would only keep for two days or so. My great aunt used to sell curry pastes in the market. Her husband, a sailor in the Thai navy, was away for months at a time. He knew that it was always a problem to prepare and keep curry paste on board, so he developed a technique to make a paste that could be dried and stored for use at a later date. He subsequently developed this into a business under the brand name Tan Jai. Their first customer was the Thai navy! Later, it became hugely popular with Thai students going abroad to study. Sadly, the brand no longer exists, although this type of product is widely available. In the West, only the best-known curries (green, red, massaman and penang) are found, but these recipes will show you how to make your own.

how to make authentic thai curry pastes

The preparation of the curry paste is the same for each curry. The ingredients should be ground using a pestle and mortar. Start with the hardest ingredient then add the other ingredients one at a time. I usually start with the chillies and sea salt – the coarse salt helps to cut through the chilli skin. As you add each ingredient, check the aroma of the paste to see how the new ingredient is balancing with the previous ones. This will ensure that you don't add too much or too little of any ingredient. You are aiming for a harmonious blend with no one flavour dominating.

Any leftover paste will keep in the fridge for two or three days. The best way to keep it fresh is to wrap it in clingfilm and place it in an airtight container. You can also freeze your curry pastes – they may lose a little flavour but they will still taste better than shop-bought pastes. Wrap in two-tablespoon portions so you can use as needed.

With practice, you can expect to grind a curry paste in about thirty minutes. It is hard work, but it can be a great stress-buster and the results are definitely worth it. The alternative is to use a blender. This will produce inferior pastes, but they will probably still be better than ready-made ones. If you do decide to use a blender, lubricate the ingredients with water rather than oil or you will end up with a gluey ball.

If dried red chillies are required, always prepare them in this way: slice lengthways, remove the seeds, cut into 1cm pieces, soak until soft, then leave to dry before grinding.

For the eight key curry pastes, I have given the amount of garlic and shallot by weight, not quantity, since sizes vary widely. This way, you can reproduce the balance of flavours exactly as I make it, and then adjust as necessary to suit your own taste.

Right: Garlic

curry paste recipes

Originally, each curry paste would have come from a different area of Thailand, with the ingredients determined by what grew in the local area. Nowadays all types of curry are available all over Thailand. The main basis of every meal for Thai people is rice and now they can choose which curry they like to eat with it. In my family home, my mother made green curry often, which is probably why myself and most of my immediate family still all love green curry – and for people entering the family, learning how to cook green curry is essential.

green curry paste

(gaeng keow wan)

Makes roughly 20 tablespoons

100g (roughly 50–60) small fresh green
   chillies
1 teaspoon sea salt
70g shallots, peeled and finely chopped
80g garlic, peeled and finely chopped
3 tablespoons finely chopped galangal
4 lemongrass stalks, finely chopped
1 tablespoon finely chopped kaffir lime peel
1 teaspoon finely chopped coriander root
2 tablespoons white peppercorns
1 tablespoon coriander seeds, dry-fried
1 tablespoon cumin seeds, dry-fried
1 tablespoon shrimp paste

red curry paste

(gaeng pet)

Makes roughly 28 tablespoons

10 large dried red chillies
20g shallots, peeled and finely chopped
40g garlic, peeled and finely chopped
2 tablespoons chopped galangal
4 lemongrass stalks, finely chopped
2 teaspoons finely chopped kaffir lime peel
1 tablespoon finely chopped coriander root
1 teaspoon white peppercorns
2 teaspoons coriander seeds
1 teaspoon cumin seeds
1 tablespoon shrimp paste

massaman curry paste

(gaeng massaman)

Makes roughly 25 tablespoons

7 large dried red chillies
1 teaspoon sea salt
30g shallots, peeled and finely chopped
40g garlic, peeled and finely chopped
2 tablespoons finely chopped galangal,
   dry-fried until brown
4 lemongrass stalks, finely chopped and
   dry-fried until brown
2 tablespoons finely chopped coriander root
1 tablespoon white peppercorns
1 tablespoon coriander seeds, dry-fried
1 tablespoon cumin seeds, dry-fried
8 whole cardamom pods, dry-fried, husks
   removed and seeds scraped out
1 small nutmeg, dry-fried, break the shell
   off and use the meat inside
½ teaspoon ground cinnamon
8 cloves, dry-fried
1 tablespoon shrimp paste

penang curry paste

(gaeng penang)

Makes roughly 12 tablespoons

5 large dried red chillies
½ teaspoon sea salt
20g shallots, peeled and finely chopped
40g garlic, peeled and finely chopped
1 tablespoon finely chopped galangal
2 lemongrass stalks, finely chopped
1 tablespoon finely chopped kaffir lime peel
1 tablespoon finely chopped coriander root
1 teaspoon white peppercorns
2 teaspoons coriander seeds, dry-fried
   until brown
1 teaspoon cumin seeds, dry-fried
   until brown
2 tablespoons roasted peanuts
1 tablespoon shrimp paste

jungle curry paste

(gaeng pa)

Makes roughly 12 tablespoons

10 large dried red chillies
1 teaspoon sea salt
20g shallots, peeled and finely chopped
40g garlic, peeled and finely chopped
2 tablespoons finely chopped galangal
4 lemongrass stalks, finely chopped
2 teaspoons coriander seeds
1 tablespoon shrimp paste

kua curry paste

(gaeng kua)

Makes roughly 14 tablespoons

10 small dried red chillies
5 large dried red chillies
1 teaspoon sea salt
20g shallots, peeled and finely chopped
50g garlic, peeled and finely chopped
1 tablespoon finely chopped galangal
4 lemongrass stalks, finely chopped
1 tablespoon finely chopped kaffir lime peel
1 tablespoon white peppercorns
1 tablespoon finely chopped fresh turmeric
  (if unavailable use the same quantity of
  ground turmeric)

home-style curry paste

(gaeng bhan)

Makes roughly 15 tablespoons

100g (roughly 70–80) small dried red
   chillies
½ teaspoon sea salt
100g garlic, peeled and finely chopped
2 tablespoons finely chopped galangal
4 lemongrass stalks, finely chopped
3 tablespoons finely chopped kaffir
   lime peel
1 tablespoon shrimp paste

orange curry paste

(gaeng som)

Makes roughly 10 tablespoons

50g (roughly 30–40) small dried red chillies
½ teaspoon sea salt
20g shallots, peeled and finely chopped
30g garlic, peeled and finely chopped
2 tablespoons finely chopped fresh turmeric
   (if unavailable use the same quantity of
   ground turmeric)

curry powder *(pong kari)*

Curry powder is a vital ingredient in several recipes in this book. This recipe makes roughly 10 tablespoons and can be stored in an airtight container for up to one year.

Makes 10 tablespoons

2 teaspoons cloves
5cm piece cinnamon stick
2 teaspoons fennel seeds
4–5 bay leaves
2 tablespoons ground cumin
5 tablespoons ground
   coriander
2 teaspoons ground turmeric
2 teaspoons paprika

1 Mix the whole herbs and spices together in a dry wok or frying pan. Stir-fry over a medium heat for 1 minute or until their aroma starts to fill the air.

2 Allow the spices to cool, then grind as finely as possible using a pestle and mortar or spice grinder. Mix in the ground spices and stir well.

what to drink with a thai curry

Most people will drink water. Others prefer black or white iced coffee or tea made very strong and sweet, which rounds off the meal, almost like a dessert. Traditionally, alcohol is only drunk with snacks, particularly with yam (a spicy Thai salad, not the starchy African vegetable!). It is not usual to drink alcohol with the main evening meal.

Left: A vendor brewing and selling fresh coffee. Not so long ago, before so many of Bangkok's canals were built over, this was a very common sight in the city. The vendor would punt his boat along the canals and people would order coffee from their porches on the canal side. Today, this still takes place, but it's mostly in the far suburbs of Bangkok where the extensive network of canals and rivers is still in everyday use.
Right: Hot tea makes a good accompaniment to curry; jasmine tea is the most popular choice.

street food

My family home is in the centre of Bangkok, near Silom Road. When I was young, it was a quiet residential area with pleasant houses and large, leafy gardens. Now it has been redeveloped into high-rise offices and apartments. This has naturally increased the number of workers and residents who need to be fed. There are now many roadside food stalls selling all manner of food.

In this area, the stallholders start work at around 4am, preparing breakfast: rice soup, freshly squeezed fruit juices, fresh fruit, coffee and, of course, curry with steamed rice. Generally, the cooks on the curry stalls will begin by preparing a big pot of one type of curry, then move onto the next. Come lunchtime, they will have a selection of at least ten different curries.

The food is served as quickly as any Western fast-food outlet, and small tables are set out on the pavement. Much is sold as takeaways to be eaten later, either at the office or at home for dinner. Lunch is generally over by 2pm when the stalls are cleaned up and packed away. The cooks then go to market to buy fresh meat, vegetables and other ingredients for the following day. Their working day is just as long as that of the office workers they feed.

Right: A selection of ready-made curries at a street stall.

snacks and
one-dish
meals

pork satay with peanut curry sauce (*moo satay*)

Satay was introduced from Malaysia – I remember when I was young the people selling satay on street stalls were never Thai! But satay is now synonymous with Thai food. You can make these with chicken, beef, pork or king prawns. You can also serve thin slices of white bread which can also be dipped into the peanut sauce.

Serves 4–6

450g lean boneless pork, cut
  lengthways into strips about
  2cm wide
2 tablespoons oil
2 tablespoons palm sugar

for the curry paste marinade
2 teaspoons coriander seeds,
  dry-fried
2 teaspoons cumin seeds,
  dry-fried
1 lemongrass stalk, finely sliced
1 tablespoon finely sliced
  galangal
1 teaspoon chopped kaffir
  lime peel
1 teaspoon ground turmeric
1 teaspoon salt

for the dipping sauce
2 tablespoons peanut oil
1 tablespoon Penang Curry
  Paste (see page 41)
100ml coconut milk
100ml chicken stock
1 tablespoon sugar
1 teaspoon salt
2 tablespoons lime juice
150g roasted peanuts, crushed

Wooden skewers, soaked in
cold water for 30 minutes

1 First make the marinade. Place the coriander seeds in a mortar and grind to a powder, then add the other ingredients in turn, grinding each one into the mixture to form a paste.

2 Place the pork, marinade, oil and palm sugar in a bowl, mix thoroughly, cover and leave to marinate in the fridge for 3–5 hours.

3 To make the dipping sauce, heat the oil in a pan. Add the curry paste, stir well and cook for few seconds. Stir in the coconut milk, stock, sugar, salt and lime juice and stir to blend. Cook for 2 minutes, stirring constantly. Add the peanuts, stirring, then pour the sauce into a bowl and set aside.

4 Thread two pieces of marinated pork onto each skewer, then grill or barbecue the satays for about 5 minutes on each side until the meat is cooked through. Serve with the peanut curry dipping sauce.

spicy beef balls (*nua tod*)

This is a quick, easy dish, the equivalent of a Thai burger mixed with curry paste. It would be served with rice in Thailand, but could also be served with pasta, or in a wrap with salad.

Serves 4–6

450g minced beef
1 large onion, finely chopped
1 tablespoon Massaman Curry
   Paste (see page 41)
2 eggs, beaten
2 tablespoons fish sauce
½ teaspoon salt
1 teaspoon sugar
3 tablespoons unsalted peanuts,
   chopped
oil, for deep-frying
lemon wedges, to serve

1 Place all the ingredients, except the oil, in a large bowl and mix well until the mixture is smooth. Wet your hands and shape the mixture into golf ball-size rounds. Set aside.

2 Heat the oil in a wok or deep pan. Prepare a tray lined with kitchen paper to drain the beef balls. Lower the balls, a few at a time, into the hot oil and deep-fry until golden brown. Remove and drain on kitchen paper. Serve hot with lemon wedges.

stir-fried beef noodles with curry paste
(mee sua)

Noodles were introduced into Thai cuisine from China some time ago. The Chinese way was to serve them quite plain, but they are more spicy now and most definitely Thai! This dish is a fusion of Chinese and Muslim tastes, originating in the South of Thailand.

Serves 4–6

2 tablespoons oil
4 small garlic cloves, finely
  chopped
1 tablespoon Red Curry Paste
  (see page 40)
450g beef fillet steak, thinly
  sliced
5 nests of egg noodles, soaked
  in cold water for 15 minutes
  and drained
2 tablespoons fish sauce
2 tablespoons light soy sauce
110g beansprouts
2 carrots, cut into fine
  matchsticks
2 large fresh red chillies,
  diagonally sliced
2 spring onions, chopped into
  2.5cm pieces

1 Heat the oil in a wok, add the garlic and stir-fry until golden.

2 Add the curry paste and stir well.

3 Add the beef and cook for about 5 minutes, stirring well.

4 Add the remaining ingredients, and cook for a few minutes more. Mix well, then serve.

thai fried noodles with crab *(mee pad boo)*

In Thailand this would be cooked with fresh crab meat. If that is not available, you can use frozen or canned crab meat, which can be found all over the world. This dish can also be served cold, which makes it a great option for preparing ahead and enjoying as a light summer lunch.

Serves 4–6

4 tablespoons oil
1 tablespoon Massaman Curry
   Paste (see page 41)
2 large eggs
225g thin rice noodles, soaked
   in water for 30 minutes and
   drained
4 spring onions, finely sliced
225g fresh white crabmeat,
   shredded
110g beansprouts
4 tablespoons fish sauce
2 tablespoons sugar
2 tablespoons chopped roasted
   peanuts
4 tablespoons lime juice
coriander leaves, to garnish

1 Heat the oil in a wok or frying pan, then stir in the curry paste. Break the eggs into the wok, cook for 1 minute and stir.

2 Add the noodles, stir well, then add the remaining ingredients in order, stirring well between each addition. Ladle onto a plate, garnish with coriander and serve.

spicy crispy noodles *(mee krop)*

Mee krop has a sweet taste and is very popular in America; it is always on the menu in Thai restaurants there and is eaten as a dish in its own right, whereas in Thailand it would be served alongside a curry. Dried shrimp (*gung haeng*) is a dry, salty flavouring that is made by boiling and peeling shrimps and leaving them out in the sun to dry.

Serves 4–6

oil, for deep-frying
225g thin rice noodles for
  the sauce
2 tablespoons oil
150g firm tofu, cut into 6mm
  cubes
75g dried shrimp (**gung haeng**)
1 tablespoon Orange Curry
  Paste (see page 43)
3 tablespoons fish sauce
2 tablespoons palm sugar
2 tablespoons tamarind
  water (see page 78)

for the garnish
2 tablespoons oil
1 egg, lightly beaten
75g beansprouts
3 spring onions, cut into
  2.5cm slivers
2 medium fresh red chillies,
  deseeded and finely sliced
20 cloves of Pickled Garlic,
  finely sliced across (see
  page 166)

1 Heat the oil in a wok over a medium heat. Add the noodles and deep-fry until golden brown and crisp. Drain and set aside.

2 To make the sauce, heat the oil in the wok, add the tofu and stir-fry until crisp. Remove and set aside.

3 Stir-fry the dried shrimp until crisp. Remove and set aside.

4 Add the curry paste to the wok, stir well, then add the fish sauce, palm sugar and tamarind water. Continue stirring until the mixture begins to caramelise. Add the reserved tofu and dried shrimp, stir quickly, then remove from the heat.

5 In another wok, heat the oil for the garnish. Drip in the egg mixture to make little ribbons of cooked egg. Drain and set aside.

6 Return the sauce to the heat and crumble in the crispy noodles, mixing gently. Transfer to a serving dish, sprinkle with the beansprouts, spring onions, cooked egg, sliced chilli and pickled garlic and serve.

curry coconut rice *(khao garee kai)*

This is a tasty dish for vegetarians with an interesting mix of ingredients. It's garnished with eggs, which is unusual in Thailand, but they work really well with the flavours here. Crispy onions are deep-fried slices of onion, which can be bought ready-made or just as easily deep-fried at home.

Serves 4–6

2 tablespoons oil
2 garlic cloves, finely chopped
2 tablespoons Home-style
   Curry Paste (see page 43)
450g long-grain rice
1 teaspoon ground turmeric
800ml coconut milk
1 teaspoon salt
5 kaffir lime leaves

for the garnish
3 hard-boiled eggs, peeled
   and quartered
1 small cucumber, thinly sliced
2 large fresh red chillies, thinly
   sliced
2 tablespoons crispy fried
   onions

1 Heat the oil in a large heavy-based pan. Add the garlic and fry over a low heat until golden brown. Add the curry paste and stir well. Add the rice and turmeric and cook for 2 minutes, stirring well.

2 Heat the coconut milk in a separate pan until almost boiling. Pour the coconut milk over the rice, stirring constantly, until the mixture comes to the boil. Add the salt and kaffir lime leaves. Cover with a tightfitting lid, reduce the heat to very low and simmer for 25 minutes.

3 Remove the lid, stir well and pile the rice onto a platter. Garnish with the eggs, cucumber and chillies and scatter the fried onion on top.

stuffed curry mussels *(mok hoy)*

My earliest memory of this dish is my grandmother serving these mussels to us when I was young. My grandmother was a princess and grew up in the Royal Palaces, where the food is always served in delicate portions, beautifully decorated and presented. This dish, with its mild curry topping, could also be served as canapés. It looks and tastes wonderful.

Serves 4–6

900g mussels
225ml coconut cream (see page 36)
1 tablespoon Red Curry Paste (see page 40)
2 eggs
2 tablespoons fish sauce
1 teaspoon sugar
4 kaffir lime leaves, finely chopped
1 large fresh red chilli, thinly sliced lengthways

1 Discard any open or broken mussels, scrub the shells with a brush and remove any beards. Soak the mussels in a bowl of cold water for 15 minutes and drain. Separate the mussel shells, discarding the halves without the flesh.

2 Stir together the coconut cream and curry paste in a bowl. Break in the eggs and stir well. Add the fish sauce, sugar and kaffir lime leaves and stir well.

3 Spread a teaspoonful of stuffing on each mussel and top with sliced red chilli. Place the mussels in a steamer over boiling water for 10 minutes. Remove and serve.

chicken penang *(penang gai)*

This dish is of Malaysian origin and has always been one of the most popular dishes in my restaurants in London and America. In fact, it is served in most Thai restaurants, both in Thailand and around the world. It is a dry curry with a mild yet rich flavour.

Serves 4–6

450ml coconut cream (see page 36)
2 tablespoons oil
2 tablespoons Penang Curry Paste (see page 41)
450g boneless chicken breast, thinly sliced
3 tablespoons fish sauce
2 teaspoons sugar
4 kaffir lime leaves, finely chopped
2 large fresh red chillies, thinly sliced
20 holy basil leaves

1 Gently heat the coconut cream in a small pan, but do not let it boil. Remove and set aside, reserving 1 tablespoon as a garnish.

2 Heat the oil in a wok or pan, add the curry paste and stir-fry briefly for about 5 minutes. Add the chicken and stir-fry until it is lightly cooked.

3 Stir in the coconut cream, fish sauce and sugar, stir well for a few minutes, then add the lime leaves, chillies and basil. Spoon into a bowl and top with the reserved coconut cream.

southern chicken curry *(gai kelek)*

Kelek is the Thai name for a fishing boat. These boats are brightly painted and the curry reflects their colours. In this dish butter is used as well as oil, a sign of the Malay Muslim influence. The curry paste contains turmeric, which is often referred to as 'The King of Herbs', and is more commonly used in the South of Thailand. As well as imparting a delicate flavour, it gives the dish its orange colour.

Serves 4–6

2 tablespoons oil

2 tablespoons butter

1.5kg whole chicken,
   quartered, then cut into
   small pieces, on the bone

2 tablespoons Kua Curry Paste
   (see page 42)

450ml coconut cream (see
   page 36)

450ml water

1 tablespoon palm sugar

3 tablespoons fish sauce

2 courgettes, thickly sliced

3 tablespoons lime juice

2 large fresh red chillies,
   finely sliced

1 Heat the oil and butter in a large saucepan and fry the chicken pieces until just golden brown.

2 Stir in the curry paste, coconut cream, water, sugar and fish sauce. Cover and cook over a low heat for 30 minutes or until the chicken is very tender.

3 Add the courgettes, lime juice and chillies. Cook for a further 5–8 minutes and serve.

chicken and lime curry (*gaeng gai ma-now*)

A refreshing dish that is cooked with whole limes as well as kaffir lime leaves. The lime gives the curry a sour, zingy taste. In Thailand it is often cooked with kaffir lime fruit. See page 33 for more about kaffir limes.

Serves 4–6

2 tablespoons oil
2 tablespoons Orange Curry
  Paste (see page 43)
1.3kg whole chicken, jointed
  into 8 pieces
225ml coconut cream (see
  page 36)
2 limes, halved
6 kaffir lime leaves, finely
  shredded
1 teaspoon salt
1 teaspoon sugar
coriander leaves, to garnish

1 Heat the oil in a large pan and add the curry paste. Stir over a low heat, then add the chicken and stir-fry for 3–4 minutes, ensuring that the chicken is coated with the paste.

2 Add the coconut cream, lime halves, shredded kaffir lime leaves, salt and sugar, then cover and simmer for about 30 minutes or until the chicken is tender. Garnish with the coriander and serve.

black pepper chicken curry (gaeng gai prik thai dum)

Black pepper grows easily all over Thailand. My mother always used a lot of black pepper in her curries. It gives a different type of 'heat' to that which you get when using chilli, so this dish is an interesting one to try.

Serves 4–6

225ml coconut cream (see
  page 36)
2 tablespoons black
  peppercorns, crushed
2 tablespoons finely chopped
  ginger, ground to a paste
2 tablespoons finely chopped
  garlic, ground to a paste
½ teaspoon salt
2 tablespoons finely chopped
  fresh coriander stems
2 tablespoons lime juice
900g boneless chicken breast,
  cut into 1cm cubes

for the curry
3 tablespoons oil
1 large onion, chopped
1 tablespoon Green Curry
  Paste (see page 40)
1 large tomato, chopped
225ml water
2 tablespoons fish sauce
1 teaspoon sugar

1 Mix together the coconut cream, peppercorns, ginger, garlic, salt, coriander, lime juice and chicken in a non-metallic bowl. Cover and marinate in the fridge for 1 hour.

2 To make the curry, heat the oil in a wok, fry the onion for about 3 minutes until golden brown, then stir in the curry paste and chopped tomato. Reduce the heat and simmer for 2 minutes.

3 Add the marinated chicken mixture, together with the water, fish sauce and sugar. Bring to the boil, stirring, then reduce the heat and simmer for 20 minutes. Serve.

tamarind chicken *(gai makham)*

Tamarind water adds a sour, zesty taste to curries and other dishes, but you can use lime juice as a substitute – you'll need double the quantity, though. To make tamarind water, take a some ripe, sour tamarind fruit, remove the hard outer skin and throw it away. Soak the inner core in hot water for 15 minutes until the pulp can be squeezed to produce the water. The water is normally used immediately, but can be kept in the fridge for a few days. Some villagers in Thailand dry-fry the remaining seeds and eat with salt and sugar as a snack, but this is probably an acquired taste!

Serves 4–6

4 chicken drumsticks
4 chicken thighs
2 tablespoons tamarind water
1 tablespoon Massaman
   Curry Paste (see page 41)
1 teaspoon salt
oil, for deep-frying
2 spring onions, finely chopped,
   to garnish

1 Remove the skin from the chicken pieces. Place the pieces in a large pan and just cover with water. Bring to the boil, then cover the pan and simmer for 10 minutes or until the chicken is cooked through. Drain and cool.

2 Mix together the tamarind water, curry paste and salt. Thoroughly coat the cooled chicken, transfer to a non-metallic dish, cover and leave to marinate in the fridge for at least 3 hours.

3 Heat the oil in a frying pan and cook the chicken over a medium heat until golden brown and heated through. Drain the chicken on kitchen paper and serve warm, garnished with spring onions.

chicken curry with sour bamboo shoots *(gaeng gai normai dong)*

Here, bamboo shoots counter the sweetness of the palm sugar. Bamboo grows all over Thailand. The young shoots are dug out and the skin is removed. The young meat is then sliced and left to soak in plain water overnight, and the roots are naturally sour. Pickled bamboo is available in jars from Oriental stores. The bamboo is boiled and then pickled in vinegar, sugar and salt, giving it a sour taste. Bamboo grows very quickly in Asia, so it is often preserved in this way. As with mushrooms, some varieties are poisonous, so check first if you are tempted to try this yourself!

Serves 4–6

450ml coconut cream (see
   page 36)
2 tablespoons Red Curry Paste
   (see page 40)
1.3–1.8kg whole chicken,
   jointed into small chunks on
   the bone
450ml water
450g pickled bamboo shoots
3 tablespoons fish sauce
2 teaspoons palm sugar
5 kaffir lime leaves
2 large fresh red chillies, finely
   sliced
20 sweet basil leaves

1 Gently heat the coconut cream in a large pan, stirring well, and simmer for about 1 minute. Add the curry paste, stir, then add the chicken pieces and simmer for 15 minutes.

2 Add the water, bamboo shoots, fish sauce, palm sugar and lime leaves. Bring back to the boil, then simmer for about 20 minutes until the chicken is tender. Add the chillies and basil leaves and serve.

northeastern steamed chicken curry in banana leaf (haw nung gai)

Every part of the banana tree is used in Asia. Banana leaves are very useful for wrapping food during steaming and they also impart a subtle flavour to the food. If you can't find them, aluminium foil or small bowls can be used as a substitute in this recipe.

Serves 4–6

450g boneless chicken breasts,
   cut into small pieces
1 tablespoon Jungle Curry Paste
   (see page 42)
5 round Thai aubergines,
   quartered
5 long beans, cut into 4cm
   lengths
225g dried vermicelli noodles,
   soaked in cold water for
   30 minutes, then drained
3 tablespoons water
4 kaffir lime leaves, finely sliced
2 tablespoons fish sauce
1 teaspoon sugar
5 sprigs of coriander, finely
   chopped

6 pieces of banana leaf or
   kitchen foil, each
   approximately 20cm square
toothpicks

1 Place all the ingredients in a bowl and mix well.

2 Take 2 tablespoons of the mixture and place on a piece of banana leaf. Fold the leaf around the mix to form a pyramid, then secure with toothpicks.

3 Repeat to make six pyramids. Transfer to a steamer and steam for 8 minutes, then serve.

chicken massaman curry (*gaeng massaman gai*)

Gaeng Massaman has become one of the most popular Thai curry dishes in the world. The origins of this dish are in Southern Thailand and Malaysia. Originally the curry was cooked with chunks of beef, but now is cooked with any type of meat. The curry is generally served mild and the combination of curry, coconut milk, potatoes and nuts is very appealing to Western tastes.

Serves 4–6

3 tablespoons oil
900g chicken legs
2 tablespoons Massaman
  Curry Paste (see page 41)
450ml coconut cream (see
  page 36)
450g potatoes, peeled and cut
  into 2.5cm cubes
4 small onions, peeled and
  quartered
4 kaffir lime leaves, roughly
  torn
450ml water
3 tablespoons fish sauce
1 tablespoon palm sugar
2 tablespoons tamarind water
  (see page 78)
3 tablespoons chopped roasted
  salted peanuts
2 large fresh red chillies, finely
  sliced

1 Heat the oil in a large saucepan and fry the chicken legs until golden. Remove the chicken and set aside.

2 Reduce the heat and stir in the curry paste, then add the coconut cream and simmer for 2 minutes.

3 Return the chicken to the pan, simmer for about 10 minutes, then add the potatoes and simmer for a further 5 minutes.

4 Add the remaining ingredients, except the chillies, and cook for a final 10 minutes.

5 Add the chillies and serve.

fried crispy pheasant *(nok tod)*

This is an Eastern-style dish. Various types of pheasant are found in Thailand and they are becoming increasingly rare, however the dish could be cooked with any bird, such as chicken. Serve with sticky rice (see page 178) and Green Papaya Salad *(som tam)* (see page 170) – heaven!

Serves 4–6

2 pheasants, jointed into
*   4 pieces*
2 tablespoons Penang Curry
*   Paste (see page 41)*
1 teaspoon salt
1 teaspoon sugar
oil, for deep-frying

1 Boil the pheasant in a large pan of water for about 10 minutes or until cooked through. Drain and leave to cool. Brush the curry paste over the cooled pieces, transfer to a non-metallic dish, and sprinkle with the salt and sugar. Cover and leave to marinate in the fridge for 30 minutes.

2 Heat the oil in a heavy-based pan, add the pheasant and cook until golden brown, turning frequently.

roast duck with lychee curry (*gaeng pet yang*)

Lychees are sweet, juicy fruits that contrast wonderfully with the taste and texture of duck. This dish is generally made with the leftover duck meat from a party, a 'day after the night before' dish.

Serves 4–6

1.8kg whole duck
5 cardamom pods or bay
   leaves
5 garlic cloves, roughly
   chopped
1 tablespoon finely chopped
   coriander root
1 tablespoon dark soy sauce
1 teaspoon salt
1 teaspoon sugar
1 teaspoon ground white
   pepper
20 cloves

for the curry
450ml coconut cream (see
   page 36)
2 tablespoons Red Curry Paste
   (see page 40)
3 tablespoons fish sauce
1 teaspoon sugar
5 kaffir lime leaves
225ml water
20 fresh lychees, stoned, or
   tinned ones, drained
10 cherry tomatoes
20 sweet basil leaves

1 Clean and dry the duck and place the cardamom or bay leaves inside the cavity. Mix together all the remaining ingredients except the cloves. Spread this mixture over the duck and press the cloves into the skin. Transfer the duck to a non-metallic dish, cover and marinate in the fridge for at least 3 hours.

2 Preheat the oven to 220°C/gas mark 7. Roast the duck for 20 minutes, then reduce the heat to 180°C/gas mark 4 and cook for a further 2 hours. Remove from the oven, leave to cool, then shred the meat from the bird.

3 To make the curry, gently heat the coconut cream in a large pan. Simmer for 2 minutes, then stir in the curry paste, fish sauce, sugar and kaffir lime leaves. Simmer for 2 minutes, then add the duck meat. Bring to the boil, slowly pour in the water, and simmer for 10 minutes.

4 Add the lychees and tomatoes and simmer for a further 5 minutes. Add the basil leaves and serve.

roasted duck with green curry paste
(bet keow wan)

This is a variation I created on the famous green curry, roasting it in a 'Western way'. It could be served with pasta, potatoes or salad. For Thais it would be eaten with rice or noodles, as shown here.

Serves 4–6

6 duck thighs
2 tablespoons Green Curry
    Paste (see page 40)
½ teaspoon salt
2 teaspoons palm sugar (or
    soft brown sugar)
2 tablespoons fish sauce

1 Trim off any excess fat from the duck. Cut a few slits in each thigh.

2 Mix together the curry paste, salt, palm sugar and fish sauce. Place the duck in a shallow, non-metallic dish and rub it all over with the mixture. Cover and let it marinate in the fridge for at least 3 hours.

3 Preheat the oven to 180°C/gas mark 4. Roast the duck for 45 minutes. Serve hot or cold.

pork in red curry with pumpkin *(gaeng pet moo faengtong)*

This is a classic Thai curry that combines meat and vegetables, in this case pumpkin. Pumpkin is grown and sold all over Thailand. It is cooked in many different ways and used in curries, stir-fries, and desserts. It brings colour and texture to the curry. Any kind of pumpkin or squash will work in this dish.

Serves 4–6

2 tablespoons oil
2 tablespoons Red Curry Paste
* (see page 40)*
900g boneless pork, cut into
* thick strips*
450ml coconut milk
450ml water
450g pumpkin, peeled and cut
* into small cubes*
6 kaffir lime leaves
3 tablespoons fish sauce
1 teaspoon sugar
2 large fresh green chillies,
* thinly sliced*
10 basil leaves, to garnish

1 Heat the oil in a wok, add the curry paste and stir. Add the meat and stir-fry until golden brown. Stir in the coconut milk, then add the water and simmer for 15 minutes.

2 Add the pumpkin, lime leaves, fish sauce and sugar. Reduce the heat and simmer for a further 15 minutes. Add the chillies, stir once, then ladle into a serving dish and garnish with the basil.

roast spicy pork chops *(gadook moo yang)*

I have adapted this dish for Western tastes by keeping the pork chops whole. Traditionally in Thailand, before ovens became more common, the meat would have been slowly cooked over a barbecue, then sliced and shared around.

Serves 4–6

2 tablespoons oil

2 tablespoons light soy sauce

2 tablespoons Penang Curry
    Paste (see page 41)

2 tablespoons honey

½ teaspoon salt

1.3kg pork chops

2 limes, cut into wedges,
    to serve

1 Combine the oil, soy sauce, curry paste, honey and salt in a large bowl. Add the pork chops and stir until the chops are completely coated in the marinade. Cover and leave to marinate in the fridge for at least 3 hours.

2 Preheat the oven to 180°C/gas mark 4. Place the chops in an oiled baking dish and cook for 50 minutes. Garnish with the lime wedges and serve with rice.

stir-fried ground pork with aubergine and green curry paste (moo pad makua)

There are a number of different types of aubergine in Thailand. The tastes are similar, but the texture varies. The purple-black aubergines found in the West can be substituted in this dish, but will need longer cooking as the skin is tougher. Thai aubergines can often be found in Oriental stores.

Serves 4–6

2 tablespoons oil
1 tablespoon Green Curry
   Paste (see page 40)
225g minced pork
2 long Thai aubergines,
   thickly sliced
2 tablespoons bean sauce
   (see page 35)
1 tablespoon light soy sauce
1 teaspoon sugar
20 sweet basil leaves
1 large red chilli, finely sliced

1 Heat the oil in a wok, add the curry paste and stir well. Stir in the pork, then add the aubergine and stir again, cooking for about 8 minutes. Add the bean sauce, soy sauce and sugar, then stir-fry for about 3 minutes (cover the pan with a lid or foil and the steam will help it cook faster).

2 Add the basil and chilli, stir thoroughly, then ladle into a dish and serve.

spicy pork with long beans *(moo pad prik king)*

Up to a metre in length, the aptly named long bean resembles a wildly overgrown string bean (which can be used as a substitute). The long bean, however, is crunchier and cooks faster. Choose darker beans with small seeds inside the pods. Make sure you cook the beans very briefly – they should be slightly crunchy rather than soft. Long beans are grown everywhere in Thailand and are widely available in Oriental supermarkets in the West. If you can't find them, you can use French beans or haricots, which are similar.

Serves 4–6

2 tablespoons oil
1 tablespoon Red Curry Paste
   (see page 40)
225g boneless pork, finely
   sliced
225g long beans, chopped into
   2.5cm pieces
2 tablespoons fish sauce
1 teaspoon sugar
1 tablespoon ground roasted
   peanuts
4 kaffir lime leaves, finely
   chopped

1 Heat the oil in a wok, add the curry paste and stir well. Add the pork and stir-fry until just cooked, then add the long beans, fish sauce, sugar, peanuts, kaffir lime leaves.

2 Stir-fry until the beans are just cooked, then serve on a platter, with noodles if liked.

spare rib curry with bitter melon
(gaeng marak)

Bitter melon is pear shaped with a green warty skin, and is in fact an immature melon. It is sometimes compared to cucumbers but has the bitterness of chicory leaves. It can be found in most Chinese supermarkets. Use young spare ribs if you can get them because the meat is more tender.

Serves 4–6

2 tablespoons oil

2 tablespoons Kua Curry Paste
  (see page 42)

1.3 litres water

2 lemongrass stalks, cut into
  5cm lengths

5 kaffir lime leaves

3 tablespoons fish sauce

1 teaspoon salt

2 teaspoons sugar

700g spare ribs, chopped into
  3cm pieces

2 bitter melons, halved
  lengthways, then sliced
  into wedges about 3cm wide

2 spring onions, roughly
  chopped

3 coriander sprigs, finely
  chopped, to garnish

1 Heat the oil in a wok, add the curry paste and stir well. Add the water, lemongrass, kaffir lime leaves, fish sauce, salt and sugar, then bring to the boil.

2 Add the spare ribs, reduce the heat and simmer for 10–15 minutes.

3 Add the bitter melon and cook gently for a further 4–5 minutes, then add the spring onions. Garnish with coriander and serve.

northern mixed meat curry *(gaeng hoh)*

The idea behind this dish is that it uses up leftovers. Whatever remains from yesterday's dinner – curry, noodles, fried vegetables – all are combined using this method to make a new dish. *'Hoh'* is northern dialect for 'throw' – it's all thrown together!

Serves 4–6

3 tablespoons oil

2 tablespoons Red Curry Paste
  (see page 40)

225g boneless pork, cut into
  thin strips

225g beef steak, cut into thin
  strips

125ml water

110g round Thai aubergines,
  quartered

110g long beans, cut into 3cm
  pieces

110g bamboo shoots, thinly
  sliced

3 tablespoons fish sauce

1 teaspoon sugar

225g vermicelli noodles, soaked
  in cold water for 30 minutes,
  then drained

2 large fresh red chillies, finely
  sliced

20 sweet basil leaves, to
  garnish

1 Heat the oil in a wok, add the curry paste and stir. Add the meat and water, bring to the boil, then simmer for 10 minutes.

2 Add the remaining ingredients in turn and stir-fry, mixing well, for 3 minutes. Ladle into a dish and serve garnished with the basil leaves.

dry beef curry *(gaeng nua yala)*

The only liquid in this curry is the small amount of stock, so it is known as a dry curry. It is from Yala in the South of Thailand, which is a predominantly Muslim area. The origins of this dish are found in Indian cooking, which has many dry dishes. Curry doesn't have to be served with rice – this dish works well with noodles too, as shown here.

Serves 4–6

2 tablespoons oil
3 medium onions, sliced
1 tablespoon grated ginger
3 garlic cloves, crushed
1 cinnamon stick
2 tablespoons Massaman
   Curry Paste (see page 41)
900g blade or skirt steak, cut
   into small chunks
125ml beef stock
1 tablespoon tamarind water
   (see page 78)
1 teaspoon sugar
½ teaspoon salt

1 Heat the oil in a large pan, add the onions, ginger, garlic and cinnamon and stir over a low heat until the onion is soft.

2 Add the curry paste and meat, stirring to ensure the meat is well coated. Add the stock, tamarind water, sugar and salt, then cover and cook over a low heat for 1 hour or until the meat is tender. Remove the cinnamon stick before serving. Serve with noodles or rice.

grilled beef curry with figs (gaeng madua nua yang)

In Thailand, this curry is made with a fruit that looks and tastes similar to a fig but is a little smaller. This fruit is called *madua*, and is from the same family as the fig. The Thai fruit is less sweet than the European varieties and is normally eaten cooked. I haven't been able to find it in the West, so I've adapted this recipe to incorporate figs instead. I always try and reinvent curries using local ingredients.

Serves 4–6

450ml coconut cream (see
    page 36)
2 tablespoons Home-style Curry
    Paste (see page 43)
450g tender beef fillet, grilled,
    then cut into thick slices
225g fresh figs, quartered
1 tablespoon finely sliced
    krachai (see page 33)
3 tablespoons fish sauce
1 teaspoon sugar
6 kaffir lime leaves
450ml water
2 large fresh red chillies, finely
    sliced

1 Heat the coconut cream in a large pan, stirring constantly for 2 minutes, then add the curry paste and stir for a further 2 minutes. Add the remaining ingredients, except the chilli, in turn. Bring to the boil and simmer for 3 minutes. Add the chillies, stir again and serve.

lamb and okra curry (*gaeng kachiap kaek*)

It is unusual to find curries cooked with okra in Thailand – their origins are from Indian food. As okra is not widely grown in Thailand, we would often use a fruit called *grajiab* instead of okra. There are a number of different varieties of *grajiab*. Some are used as a vegetable, and others are used for making juice and are believed to be a health drink. As it is not an easy ingredient to find in the West, this recipe uses okra instead.

Serves 4–6

3 tablespoons oil
2 tablespoons Kua Curry
   Paste (see page 42)
900g lean lamb, cut into 2.5cm
   cubes
4 tablespoons water
225g okra, washed, trimmed
   but left whole
2 tablespoons fish sauce
2 teaspoons sugar
coriander leaves, chopped, to
   garnish

1 Heat the oil in a frying pan, add the curry paste and stir well. Add the lamb, stirring to coat. Add the water and stir well. Cover and cook on a low heat for 15–20 minutes until the lamb is tender.

2 Add the okra, fish sauce and sugar and cook on a high heat for about 3 minutes. Garnish with the coriander and serve.

massaman lamb curry *(massaman kaek)*

All my Western friends love this one. It's spicy but doesn't have too much chilli. You can eat it with bread, Indian style. The name Massaman comes from the Thai word for Muslim. Lamb is not widely eaten by Thai people, as the smell of the meat is not liked. In this recipe, red shallots are used, which cover the smell.

Serves 4–6

450ml coconut cream (see
page 36)
2 tablespoons oil
2 tablespoons Massaman Curry
Paste (see page 41)
900g lamb, cut into 3cm cubes
2 tablespoons tamarind water
(see page 78)
2 teaspoons sugar
3 tablespoons fish sauce
450ml stock or water
6 small potatoes, quartered
4 tablespoons whole roasted
peanuts
6 small shallots

1 Gently warm the coconut cream in a small pan until it just starts to separate. Remove from the heat and set aside.

2 Heat the oil in a wok, add the curry paste and stir well. Add half the warmed coconut cream and cook for 2–3 minutes, stirring all the time. Add the lamb and stir to coat in the curry sauce. Add the tamarind water, sugar, fish sauce and the remainder of the coconut cream, stirring constantly. Add half the stock, simmer gently for 10 minutes, stirring well, then add the remaining stock and simmer for a further 10 minutes, stirring occasionally.

3 Add the potatoes and simmer for 5 minutes. Add the peanuts and cook for a further 5 minutes, then finally stir in the shallots and cook for another 5 minutes. Ladle into a large dish and serve.

fish

southern thai fish curry *(gaeng pet pla)*

I first tasted this dish in Phuket when I went there on a trip with friends from art school. We all stayed at the beach with local people and they cooked this curry for us. Turmeric is widely used in cooking in the south of Thailand and gives southern dishes a distinctive colour.

Serves 4–6

2 tablespoons oil
2 tablespoons Red Curry Paste
   (see page 40)
450ml coconut milk
450ml fish or vegetable stock,
   or water
½ teaspoon ground turmeric
3 tablespoons fish sauce
1 tablespoon sugar
1 tablespoon tamarind water
   (see page 78)
450g monkfish, hoki or red
   snapper fillet, cut
   into large chunks
3 tomatoes, quartered
1 red pepper, cored, deseeded
   and chopped
1 green pepper, cored,
   deseeded and chopped
Few coriander leaves, to garnish

1 Heat the oil in a large wok, add the curry paste and stir well. Stir in the coconut milk, stock or water, turmeric, fish sauce, sugar and tamarind water, and simmer for 5 minutes.

2 Add the fish and simmer for 6–8 minutes. Stir in the tomatoes and peppers, simmer over a low heat for about 10 minutes until thickened. Ladle into a serving bowl and garnish with coriander.

haddock with green curry sauce *(keo wan pla)*

Fish is my favourite food. On a trip to Ko Samui, I ordered this dish in a small restaurant on the beach and really enjoyed it. Any fish can be used, but make sure you don't stir it, as you may break up the fish.

Serves 4–6

450ml coconut cream (see
  page 36)
1 teaspoon salt
2 tablespoons Green Curry
  Paste (see page 40)
1 tablespoon palm sugar
4 haddock fillets, each weighing
  about 150g
10 kaffir lime leaves, finely
  sliced
2 large fresh red chillies, thinly
  sliced

1 Gently heat the coconut cream in a large frying pan, add the salt and stir in the green curry paste, mixing well. Add the palm sugar, stirring constantly. Add the haddock and kaffir lime leaves, then bring slowly to simmering point.

2 Reduce the heat, cover and poach the fish for 10–15 minutes, depending on its thickness. Transfer the fish to warmed plates, garnish with chillies and serve.

fish curry with papaya *(pla gaeng som)*

The best papayas to use for this curry are green, unripe ones that are just starting to turn yellow. Papaya grows everywhere in Thailand, even in most inhospitable surroundings. It is eaten green as a vegetable in salads, the most famous of which is Green Papaya Salad (*som tam*, see page 170). When ripe, papaya is sweet and served as a dessert fruit. It is also made into jams and sold dried and preserved.

Serves 4–6

1.1 litres water

*2 tablespoons Orange Curry
   Paste (see page 43)*

*450g monkfish fillet, cut into
   large chunks*

*1 small unripe papaya, peeled,
   deseeded and roughly sliced*

1 teaspoon salt

2 tablespoons fish sauce

1 tablespoon palm sugar

*3 tablespoons tamarind water
   (see page 78)*

*coriander leaves and slices of
   red chilli, to garnish*

1 Bring the water to the boil in a large pan, add the curry paste and stir well. Add the fish and cook gently for about 5 minutes.

2 Add the remaining ingredients, stir well and gently cook for a further 5 minutes. Serve hot, garnished with coriander and red chilli.

mackerel in red curry *(chu chee pla)*

Mackerel is a very popular fish in Thailand. It is found in every market and sold on street side stalls all over the country. This simple and satisfying curry is an ideal dish for sharing. It can be served with stir fried vegetables and rice.

Serves 4–6

4 tablespoons oil
3 mackerel fillets, cleaned
1 tablespoon Red Curry Paste
  (see page 40)
225ml coconut cream (see
  page 36)
2 tablespoons fish sauce
1 teaspoon sugar
5 kaffir lime leaves, finely sliced
2 large fresh red chillies, thinly
  sliced
20 sweet basil leaves

1 Heat 2 tablespoons of oil in a large, deep-sided frying pan, add the mackerel and fry over a medium heat for 5–7 minutes or until the fish is cooked. Remove the fish from the oil, drain on kitchen paper and set aside.

2 Heat the remaining oil in the frying pan, add the curry paste and stir well, then add the coconut cream and the remaining ingredients. Add the fish to the pan and cook for a further 2–3 minutes, stirring constantly. Ladle into a dish, add the basil leaves and serve.

curried fish balls with bamboo shoots *(gaeng p…*
lukchin pla)

Fish balls are like small round dumplings and are made from fish and flour. They are made by removing the skin from the fish and cutting the flesh into small pieces. The flesh is then pounded, mixed with a little flour, and moulded into balls. The fish skin is not discarded – it is sun-dried or deep-fried to crispen it, then added to curry or soup, or served as a side dish with chilli dip (*nam prik*). Fish balls can be bought ready prepared in Chinese stores.

Serves 4–6

2 tablespoons oil
2 tablespoons Jungle Curry
    Paste (see page 42)
450g fish balls
675ml water
3 tablespoons fish sauce
6 kaffir lime leaves
150g bamboo shoots
1 tablespoon finely sliced
    krachai (see page 33)
20 sweet basil leaves

1 Heat the oil in a large pan, add the curry paste, then add the fish balls quickly and stir-fry for 2 minutes.

2 Add the remaining ingredients in turn, stirring well, then bring to the boil. Ladle into a dish, add the basil leaves and serve.

stir-fried spicy seafood *(pad pet talay)*

Being Thai, I naturally think this is the best way in the world to cook seafood. Seafood is abundant all over Thailand and is the most popular ingredient for Thai people. *Talay* is the Thai word for sea. This dish can be a main meal if served with rice, but is often served as a snack with drinks.

Serves 4–6

3 tablespoons oil
2 medium onions, sliced
1 tablespoon Red Curry Paste
   (see page 40)
450g raw prawns, peeled and
   deveined, tails on
175g squid, cut into 6cm
   squares, and scored in
   a criss-cross fashion with a
   small knife
225g mussels, cleaned and
   debearded (discard any with
   open or broken shells)
1 large tomato, finely chopped
20 basil leaves
2 tablespoons fish sauce
1 teaspoon sugar
10 sweet basil leaves, to
   garnish

1 Heat the oil in a wok, add the onions and cook until soft. Add the curry paste and stir well. Add the seafood and cook over a high heat for 3–5 minutes.

2 Stir in the tomato, basil, fish sauce and sugar, and stir-fry for a further 3 minutes. Ladle into a serving dish, garnish with the basil leaves and serve.

steamed prawn curry in banana leaf *(haw mok kung)*

For this recipe, the traditional way to cook and present the curry is in a banana leaf cup. To make each cup, cut two 15cm circles from a banana leaf, place one on top of the other and fold round into a cup with 4cm-high sides. Secure the corners with a staple or a wooden toothpick. You need to make 4 cups for this amount of curry.

Serves 4–6

400g raw prawns, peeled,
   deveined and finely chopped
1 tablespoon Red Curry Paste
   (see page 40)
225ml coconut cream (see
   page 36)
1 teaspoon salt
1 teaspoon sugar
1 tablespoon ground roasted
   peanuts
40 sweet basil leaves
1 large fresh red chilli, finely
   sliced

2 large banana leaves
Toothpicks

1 Place the prawns, curry paste, coconut cream, salt, sugar and peanuts in a bowl and mix well. Cover and set aside in the fridge for 1 hour.

2 Place 10 basil leaves in the base of each cup. Fill each one with the cold mixture and transfer the cups to a steamer set over boiling water. Steam for 10 minutes. Remove from the steamer, garnish with chilli and serve.

spicy prawns with peppercorns *(pad cha kung)*

This is on my new menu in Ko Samui. Peppercorns are one of the ingredients I grow in my kitchen garden there. Fresh peppercorns are more expensive in the West, where you won't find this kind of dish on the menu so often. The peppercorns add a bite to the prawns and their crunchiness contrasts with the soft flesh of the prawns. Unfortunately there is no substitute for *krachai*. If you can't find it, you could use sliced young ginger but this will give a different taste.

Serves 4–6

3 tablespoons oil
1 tablespoon Kua Curry Paste
  (see page 42)
900g raw king prawns, peeled
  and deveined
3 tablespoons fish sauce
1 teaspoon sugar
1 tablespoon finely sliced
  krachai (see page 33)
50g fresh green peppercorns

1 Heat the oil in a wok, add the curry paste, stir well, then add the remaining ingredients in turn, stirring quickly. Cook over a high heat for 2 minutes, then ladle into a dish and serve.

pineapple curry with mussels *(gaeng kua hoy)*

How lucky we are in Thailand to have a ready supply of seafood as well as fruit and vegetables. Pineapples are widely grown in the South of Thailand and I love this combination of mussels and pineapple. This is another dish that is very popular in my restaurant in Miami. It used to be a special, but people kept asking for it, so now it's on the menu every day. The contrast of tastes and textures in this dish is very refreshing.

Serves 4–6

900g fresh mussels
450ml coconut cream (see
  page 36)
2 tablespoons Orange Curry
  Paste (see page 43)
225ml water
2 tablespoons fish sauce
1 tablespoon palm sugar
1 tablespoon tamarind water
  (see page 78)
400g prepared pineapple, cut
  into small cubes
20 sweet basil leaves

1 Discard any open or broken mussels, scrub the shells with a brush and remove any beards. Soak the mussels in cold water for 15 minutes, then drain.

2 Heat the coconut cream in a large pan, add the curry paste and stir over a medium heat for 2 minutes.

3 Slowly add the water, bring to the boil, then stir in the fish sauce, palm sugar and tamarind water. Add the mussels and pineapple and simmer for about 2 minutes. Add the basil and mix well before serving.

spicy squid *(pad pet pla muk)*

Squid is very popular in Thailand. If you are at the seaside in Thailand at night, you will usually see a row of fishing boats on the horizon with bright lights shining on the sea to attract the squid. If you can find it, fresh squid cooks more quickly and has a less rubbery texture. Serve with rice and wedges of lime to make a main course.

Serves 4–6

*700g squid, cut into large
  pieces and scored in a
  criss-cross fashion with the tip
  of a knife*
2 tablespoons lime juice
2 tablespoons oil
*1 tablespoon Red Curry Paste
  (see page 40)*
2 tablespoons fish sauce
2 teaspoons sugar
1 medium onion, finely sliced
*2 large fresh red chillies, finely
  sliced*
20 sweet basil leaves

1 Place the squid in a bowl with the lime juice. Cover and leave to marinate for 1 hour in the fridge.

2 Heat the oil in a wok, add the curry paste and stir well. Add the squid and cook over a moderate heat for 2 minutes, then add the fish sauce, sugar, onion and chillies. Stir well for 2 minutes, add the basil leaves and serve.

crab with curry powder *(boo pad pong kari)*

The origins of this dish are a mix of Malay, Chinese, and Indian – the use of curry powder is quite unusual in Thai food. This dish looks striking on the plate with the crab claws creating an impressive spectacle.

Serves 4–6

900g fresh whole crab
  (uncooked)
2 tablespoons oil
3 garlic cloves, crushed
2 tablespoons Curry Powder
  (see page 44)
2 eggs
4 whole spring onions, cut into
  5cm pieces
1 tablespoon finely chopped
  ginger
2 tablespoons fish sauce
1 tablespoon light soy sauce
1 teaspoon sugar
2 large fresh red chillies, thinly
  sliced
coriander leaves, to garnish

1 Scrub the crab well. Pull back the apron from the underbelly and snap off. Twist off the legs and claws. Pull the body apart and remove the feathery gills and internal organs. Use a cleaver to chop the body into 4 pieces. Crack the claws with a good hit using the back of the cleaver.

2 Heat the oil in a wok, add the garlic and fry until golden brown. Add the curry powder and eggs, stir well, then add the crab and stir-fry for 2–3 minutes.

3 Add the spring onions, ginger, fish sauce, soy sauce, sugar and chillies and cook for 4–5 minutes. Garnish with coriander and serve.

sweet potato and mushroom curry *(gaeng man gap het)*

The sweet richness of this red tuber complements the hot and sour flavours of southeast Asia. Sweet potato grows easily in Thailand and is often used in vegetarian food, but does not generally feature in mainstream Thai food. It is also used in desserts, and grilled to sell as a snack.

Serves 4–6

450ml water
2 tablespoons Jungle Curry
   Paste (see page 42)
450g sweet potato, peeled and
   cut into 2.5cm cubes
110g oyster mushrooms,
   washed and separated
6 kaffir lime leaves, roughly torn
2 tablespoons light soy sauce
1 teaspoon sugar

1 Bring the water to the boil in a pan, add the curry paste and stir well. Add the potato, reduce the heat and simmer for 10 minutes.

2 Add the remaining ingredients, cook for a further 3 minutes and serve.

southern vegetable curry (*gaeng liang*)

This curry paste is particular to this dish. It doesn't use many ingredients and is quick to make. White peppercorns have a milder taste than black ones. The sweet basil leaf traditionally used is *bai meng luk* and is only grown in certain areas. It needs to be eaten very fresh, and does not travel well. Any vegetables can be used according to availability and your tastes.

Serves 4–6

900ml water
110g courgettes, cut into 2.5cm
    cubes
110g pumpkin, cut into 2.5cm
    cubes
110g baby sweetcorn, sliced
    diagonally in half
110g oyster mushrooms,
    separated
2 medium tomatoes, quartered
20 sweet basil leaves

for the curry paste
½ teaspoon white peppercorns
4 small dried red chillies
½ teaspoon salt
6 small Thai shallots

1 First make the curry paste. Pound the peppercorns in a stone mortar to a powder, then add the chillies and pound again. Add the salt and shallots and pound the mixture into a paste.

2 Bring the water to the boil in a pan and stir in the curry paste. Add the vegetables, reduce the heat and simmer for 20 minutes, stirring occasionally. Add the basil leaves and serve.

papaya curry *(gaeng luang)*

This is a very hot curry from southern Thailand that is given its bright yellow colour by the fresh turmeric. Local people add yellow chillies to the sauce for extra heat and colour. It's usually made with prawns but this is my vegetarian version. Unripe papayas are treated like vegetables in Thailand. They have green skin and flesh and are used in hot dishes and salads, whereas ripe papayas have orange flesh and are eaten as fruit.

Serves 4–6

900ml water
900g green papaya, peeled,
   deseeded and cut
   into 3cm slices
1 tablespoon tamarind water
   (see page 78)
4 medium tomatoes, quartered
1 teaspoon salt

for the yellow curry paste
4 small dried red chillies
½ teaspoon salt
1 tablespoon finely chopped
   lemongrass
1 tablespoon finely chopped
   garlic
2 teaspoons finely chopped
   fresh turmeric

1 First make the curry paste. Pound the chillies in a stone mortar, then add the remaining ingredients, pounding each one in turn, until the mixture forms a paste.

2 Bring the water to the boil in a pan and stir in the curry paste. Add the papaya, tamarind water, tomatoes and salt and simmer for 20 minutes or until the papaya is soft, then serve.

stir-fried spicy cauliflower and long beans (pad pet dok galam)

We Thais don't like our vegetables to be too soft. They should be quickly stir-fried to keep the texture crunchy, especially cauliflowers, which are a recent introduction to Thailand and grown mainly in the north of the country. Until recently they were very expensive and consequently they are still not widely used in Thai food. For more about long beans, see page 101.

Serves 4–6

2 tablespoons oil
3 garlic cloves, finely chopped
1 tablespoon Red Curry Paste
   (see page 40)
450g cauliflower, cut into florets
125ml water
225g long beans, cut into 3cm
   lengths
2 tablespoons light soy sauce
1 teaspoon sugar
2 tablespoons lime juice

1 Heat the oil in a wok and fry the garlic until crispy, then remove and set aside. Stir the curry paste into the oil, then add the cauliflower and water and simmer for 3 minutes.

2 Add the beans, soy sauce and sugar and stir-fry for 2 minutes, stirring constantly. Stir in the lime juice, then transfer to a dish. Garnish with the crispy garlic and serve.

vegetable curry *(gaeng pet pak)*

This curry is very popular with vegetarians. The essence of this dish is the mix of the vegetables, which should not be cooked for too long so they retain their crunchy texture. Broccoli, pumpkin or any crunchy vegetable can be used.

Serves 4–6

2 tablespoons oil
2 tablespoons Red Curry Paste
  (see page 40)
450ml coconut cream (see
  page 36)
450ml vegetable stock
6 long beans, cut into 2.5cm
  pieces
6 baby sweetcorn, cut into
  2.5cm pieces
6 round Thai aubergines,
  quartered
1 large carrot, cut into
  matchsticks
2 large fresh red or green
  chillies, sliced
4 kaffir lime leaves, roughly
  chopped
2 teaspoons salt
2 teaspoons sugar
2 tablespoons light soy sauce
30 sweet basil leaves

1 Heat the oil in a pan and stir in the curry paste. Add the coconut cream, mixing well, then stir in the stock.

2 Add all the vegetables, the chillies, lime leaves, salt, sugar and soy sauce. Stir well, then cook briefly until the vegetables are cooked to your taste. Ladle into a bowl, stir in the basil leaves and serve.

stuffed omelette (*matabak*)

This dish was originally a southern Thai Muslim speciality. As with many Southern Thai dishes, the origins are Indian. *Matabak* is mainly sold in Muslim restaurants or in road-side 'roti stalls'. It can also be served with meat fillings.

Serves 4–6

3 eggs
1 tablespoon light soy sauce
2 tablespoons oil

for the filling

2 tablespoons oil
2 teaspoons finely chopped
  garlic
50g onions, finely chopped
50g fresh or frozen peas
50g tomatoes, finely chopped
50g carrots, finely chopped
50g straw mushrooms, finely
  chopped
50g peppers, finely chopped
2 teaspoons Curry Powder (see
  page 44)
2 tablespoons light soy sauce
½ teaspoon sugar
½ teaspoon ground black
  pepper

1 First make the filling. Heat the oil in a pan and fry the garlic until golden. Add the remaining ingredients in turn, cooking for about 5–10 minutes and stirring constantly. Remove from the heat and set aside.

2 Beat the eggs, add the soy sauce and mix well. Heat the oil in a wok, tilting it to coat the entire surface with the oil.

3 Pour in the egg and tip the wok to spread evenly. When the egg has dried, pour the filling into the centre. Fold in the sides of the omelette to make a square parcel. Cook briefly to warm through the filling, then lift carefully onto a dish and serve.

pineapple curry *(gaeng kua sapparot)*

If you buy a pineapple and find it is too sour to eat on its own, this is a great way to use it and bring out the flavour. Pineapples are grown all over Thailand and their size and taste varies according to where they are grown – they are large and juicy in Chantaburi, and small and sweet in the south.

Serves 4–6

2 tablespoons oil
2 tablespoons Kua Curry Paste
   (see page 42)
450ml coconut cream (see
   page 36)
225ml water
2 tablespoons light soy sauce
½ teaspoon salt
2 tablespoons lime juice
4 kaffir lime leaves, thinly sliced
1 fresh pineapple, trimmed and
   cut into small cubes
Red chilli, finely chopped, for
   garnish

1 Heat the oil in a pan and fry the curry paste, stirring well. Stir in the coconut cream. Add the water, slowly bring to the boil, then add the soy sauce, salt, lime juice, lime leaves and pineapple.

2 Simmer for 3 minutes, then transfer to a bowl, garnish with chilli and serve.

stir-fried aubergine with green curry paste and bean sauce *(makua pat keow wan)*

This curry can be made with any aubergines, the common large purple ones as seen on the right or Thai aubergines, which are not as familiar to Westerners. They are available in Oriental supermarkets and are round, pale green and about 2.5cm in diameter. If the purple ones are used, they should be cooked until soft, whereas Thai aubergines are better left *al dente*. The bean sauce used in this dish can be black bean or yellow bean and gives the dish a salty taste to contrast with the curry flavours.

Serves 4–6

2 tablespoons oil
2 tablespoons Green Curry
   Paste (see page 40)
450g aubergines, cut into
   2.5cm cubes
4 tablespoons vegetable stock
   or water
75g red pepper, cored,
   deseeded and cut
   lengthways into thin strips
1 tablespoon bean sauce
1 tablespoon light soy sauce
1 tablespoon sugar
2 large fresh red chillies, thinly
   sliced
20 holy basil leaves

1 Heat the oil in a pan and stir in the curry paste. Stir in the aubergine and stock, and cook until the aubergine begins to soften (about 5 minutes).

2 Add the remaining ingredients, stirring constantly. Cook for 1 minute and serve.

chickpea curry (*gaeng pet tua*)

Chickpeas are not commonly used in Thai cooking. They are most likely to be found in dishes from the south of Thailand, where the influence of Indian food is more apparent. I first ate this dish in a temple where I spent some time as a monk – the more spiritual of the monks were all vegetarian.

Serves 4–6

2 tablespoons oil

2 tablespoons Massaman Curry Paste (see page 41)

450ml coconut cream (see page 36)

450ml water

2 medium potatoes, peeled and cut into 2.5cm cubes

225g dried chickpeas, soaked overnight, or use tinned

2 small onions, cut into 2.5cm cubes

2 large fresh red chillies, cut lengthways into thin slivers

2 tablespoons light soy sauce

½ teaspoon salt

1 tablespoon sugar

1 Heat the oil in a pan and stir in the curry paste. Stir in the coconut cream, mixing well, then add the remaining ingredients in turn.

2 Bring to the boil and simmer for about 15 minutes until the potatoes and chickpeas are cooked. Transfer to a dish and serve.

green curry with young coconut (gaeng keow wan maprow)

Young coconuts differ from ripe coconuts in the texture of the flesh. You can find young green coconuts in oriental stores, and they are also available tinned. You need two young green coconuts for this recipe. Cut them open, drain off the coconut water (a refreshing drink when chilled) and use the coconut flesh. Traditionally this curry is served inside the coconut shell.

Serves 4–6

2 tablespoons oil
2 garlic cloves, finely chopped
2 tablespoons Green Curry
   Paste (see page 40)
450ml coconut cream (see
   page 36)
450ml water
175g young coconut flesh, thinly
   sliced (see above)
2 large fresh red chillies, sliced
   diagonally into thin ovals
1 teaspoon salt
8 round Thai aubergines,
   quartered
2 teaspoons sugar
20 sweet basil leaves

1 Heat the oil in a large pan, add the garlic and fry until golden brown. Stir in the curry paste, mixing well. Add the coconut cream and keep stirring for 2 minutes.

2 Slowly add the water and bring to the boil, stirring constantly. Add the sliced coconut, chillies, salt, aubergines and sugar. Simmer for about 3 minutes until the aubergines are cooked. Stir in the basil leaves just before pouring into a bowl and serve.

boiled egg curry *(gaeng kai)*

Served with bread this makes a good breakfast or lunch dish.

Serves 4–6

2 tablespoons oil
5 small shallots, finely sliced
3 garlic cloves, finely sliced
2 tablespoons Massaman Curry
   Paste (see page 41)
125ml water
3 cardamom pods
5 cloves
5cm piece of cinnamon stick
125ml coconut milk
2 teaspoons salt
1 tablespoon palm sugar
6 hard-boiled eggs, peeled and
   halved
2 large fresh red chillies, sliced

for the garnish
1 tablespoon deep-fried onions
2 large fresh red chillies, finely
   sliced
coriander leaves

1 Heat the oil in a pan and fry the shallots and garlic for 2 minutes. Stir in the curry paste, mixing well.

2 Add the water and the remaining ingredients in turn. Simmer gently for 10 minutes. Garnish with the deep-fried onions, chillies and coriander leaves, and serve.

pickles and
salads

fresh vegetable pickle *(ajart)*

Ajart should be treated like a side dish. It goes particularly well with dry or rich curries that do not have vegetables included, such as Chicken Massaman Curry (page 85), Massaman Lamb Curry (page 112) and Curry Coconut Rice (page 64). *Ajart* is also used as a dip for savoury snacks. This recipe serves 4–6 people. It doesn't keep well as the vegetables go soft; eat on the same day.

Serves 4–6

225ml rice vinegar
4 tablespoons sugar
1 teaspoon salt
1 large red chilli, sliced
1 large green chilli, sliced
450g (total weight) cucumber,
*   shallots and carrots, sliced*

1 Heat the vinegar in a pan. Add the sugar and salt and stir to dissolve. Allow the mixture to cool.

2 Place the sliced vegetables in a bowl and cover with the vinegar. Set aside for 30 minutes, then serve.

pickle recipes

Various fruits and vegetables can be pickled, either in salted water or in a mixture of salt, sugar and vinegar. They are used in the cooking methods of some of the curry recipes in this book and are also good as accompaniments to the curries – it's largely a matter of personal preference as to which ones you choose to serve! These three dishes are of Chinese origin, and originally would have been eaten with plain rice. Their tastes contrast well with spicy food.

pickled garlic

(king dong)

450g garlic, peeled
450ml rice vinegar
200g sugar
2 tablespoons salt

Place the garlic cloves in a bowl, cover with water and soak for 1 hour. Drain and allow to dry for a further hour.

Heat the vinegar in a pan, add the sugar and salt and stir to dissolve. Allow the mixture to cool. Place the garlic in a preserving jar, pour the vinegar over the garlic and seal the jar.

Set aside for 3–4 weeks. Do not refrigerate until after the jar is opened.

pickled ginger

(katriam dong)

450g fresh young ginger, peeled and cut
into thin slices
450ml rice vinegar
400g sugar
2 tablespoons salt

Place the ginger in a bowl and rinse in water. Drain and set aside.

Heat the vinegar in a pan, add the sugar and salt and stir to dissolve. Allow the mixture to cool.

Place the ginger in a preserving jar, pour the vinegar over it and seal the jar. Leave for 3 weeks. Do not refrigerate until after the jar is opened.

salted eggs

(kae kem)

8 duck eggs
200g salt
675ml water

Place the eggs in their shells in a
preserving jar. Heat the salt and water in
a saucepan until the salt has dissolved.

Allow the mixture to cool, then pour
over the eggs in the jar. Seal the jar
and set aside for 3 weeks, after
which the eggs can be boiled
or fried.

spicy noodle salad with pork and prawns *(yam gueyteow)*

Because this dish is served cold it works very well as party food. I like it because I can prepare everything before the guests arrive and then enjoy the party.

Serves 4

6 lettuce leaves
225g rice stick noodles, soaked
   in warm water for 5 minutes,
   then rinsed and drained
170g fresh prawns, shelled and
   deveined
85g lean pork, finely sliced
2 garlic cloves, finely chopped
2 small fresh red chillies, finely
   chopped
2 tablespoons fish sauce
2 tablespoons lime juice
½ teaspoon sugar
115g celery, finely chopped
1 tablespoon roasted peanuts,
   ground
2 spring onions, finely sliced

1 Arrange the lettuce leaves on large platter and set aside.

2 In a pan, boil some water and, using a sieve or strainer, dip the noodles in the boiling water for a few seconds, then place in a large bowl.

3 Drop the prawns and pork in the boiling water until they are cooked, then drain and place in the bowl with the noodles.

4 Add all the remaining ingredients to the bowl, stirring well. Spoon the mixture onto the lettuce-covered platter and serve.

green papaya salad *(som tam)*

A famous dish throughout all of Thailand, *Som Tam* is now as well known as *Tom Yam* and *Pad Thai.* Originally from Isaan, the north-east of Thailand, it is now sold everywhere. It is always sold fresh. Watching it being prepared is entertaining and the taste and spiciness can be adjusted for different tastes. If prepared with soy sauce, this is suitable for vegetarians.

Serves 4

*110g green papaya, peeled
and seeds removed*
1 garlic clove
*3 small fresh red or green
chillies*
1 tablespoon roasted peanuts
*25g long beans, chopped
into 2.5cm lengths (French
beans may be substituted)*
2 tablespoons lemon juice
*3 tablespoons light soy sauce
or fish sauce*
1 teaspoon sugar
*1 medium tomato, chopped
into segments*
2 large leaves Chinese cabbage

1 Finely shred the papaya flesh with a cheese grater or chop it very finely into long, thin shreds. Set aside.

2 In a mortar, lightly pound the garlic, add the chillies, and lightly pound again. Add the peanuts and lightly pound while occasionally stirring with a spoon to prevent the resulting paste from thickening.

3 Add the long beans and slightly bruise them. Add the shredded papaya, lightly pound and stir until all the ingredients are blended together. Add the lemon juice, soy or fish sauce and sugar and stir into the mixture. Finally add the tomato, stirring once.

4 Put the cabbage leaves on a plate and turn the mixture on to them.

vegetable salad with peanut sauce *(salad kaek)*

As the Thai name suggests, this dish derives from Malaysia and Indonesia. It's a great vegetarian option.

1 First make the sauce. Heat the oil in a wok or large frying pan, and stir in the curry paste. Add the coconut milk and stir well. Add all the remaining ingredients together, continuing to stir. Cook briefly until the coconut milk comes to the boil. Remove at once from the heat.

2 To make the salad, heat the oil and deep-fry the beancurd until golden. Remove, drain and set aside.

3 Arrange all the vegetables in a salad bowl. Shell and quarter the eggs, then place them in the bowl. Thinly slice the beancurd and add to the bowl.

4 Serve the salad with the sauce, either separately or poured over the salad and tossed.

Serves 4–6

Oil, for deep-frying
2 blocks of beancurd, about
  5cm square
110g beansprouts
110g long beans, chopped into
  2.5cm lengths
1 medium tomato, thinly sliced
110g cucumber, thinly sliced
110g white cabbage, thinly
  sliced, then broken up into
  strands
2 hard-boiled eggs

for the sauce
2 tablespoons oil
1 tablespoon Red Curry Paste
  (see page 40)
450ml coconut milk
½ teaspoon salt
1 tablespoon sugar
1 teaspoon tamarind water
  (see page 78)
4 tablespoons crushed roasted
  peanuts

egg noodles and squid salad *(ba mee pla muk)*

This is another of my mother's favourites. It is quick and easy to cook – a delicious noodle dish, with the sharp, refreshing flavours of lime and chilli.

Serves 4

4 nests egg noodles
340g squid, cleaned and
   roughly chopped
170g white cabbage, roughly
   chopped
4 tablespoons fish sauce
2 tablespoons light soy sauce
1 teaspoon sugar
4 tablespoons lemon juice
2 small fresh red chillies, finely
   chopped
3 spring onions, cut into 5cm
   lengths

1 Bring a pan of water to the boil, add the noodles and simmer until they soften and separate. Remove from the water, drain and hold under cold water to stop the cooking process. Drain well again and set aside.

2 Place the squid in a pan, cover with water and bring to the boil. Remove from the water, drain and set aside.

3 Dip the cabbage in the boiling water, drain and set aside.

4 Place the noodles, squid, cabbage and all the remaining ingredients in a bowl and mix well. Turn onto a large plate and serve.

rice and noodles

rice (khao)

Rice is the all-important food in Thailand. In the Thai language the verb 'to eat' is *kin khao*, which actually means 'eat rice'. Rice is completely central to Thai food. A Thai will always start by having a plate of rice; the other dishes are to accompany the rice, not vice versa as in the West. Thais will also feel uncomfortable if they don't eat rice once a day, no matter what else they may have eaten.

Traditionally we Thais finish all the rice on our plate out of respect for the Mother Goddess of Rice and to acknowledge the hardship that farmers endure in cultivating their crop. After finishing the meal, appreciative diners will put their hands together to thank the rice for filling their stomachs.

The recipes in this section deal with various rice dishes that are popular throughout Thailand. Rice serves as a gentle introduction to Thai cuisine for the gastronomically timid and those unused to highly spiced foods.

boiled rice (khao suay)

An experienced Thai cook varies the water quantity according to the age, and thus the dryness, of the rice; the amount below is a reasonable average. An alternative to preparing rice in this way is to buy a rice cooker – they are cheap, efficient and make and keep perfect rice with absolutely no fuss or bother.

Serves 4
450g Thai fragrant rice
600ml water

1 Rinse the rice thoroughly in at least three changes of cold water, until the water runs clear. Drain the rice and put it in a heavy saucepan with the measured water. Cover and quickly bring to the boil.

2 Uncover and cook, stirring vigorously, until the water level is below that of the rice, whose surface will begin to look dry. Reduce the heat to as low as possible, cover the pan again and steam for 20 minutes.

crispy rice *(khao tang)*

If, when you are cooking rice, a mishap occurs and you are left with rice sticking to the bottom of the pan, don't worry – nothing is wasted in Thai cooking. Just follow the steps below.

rice that has stuck to the pan
oil, for deep-frying

1 Let the pan cool down and then lift out the sheet of rice and dry it. Once dry, break it into 3 or 4 pieces.

2 Heat a pan of oil for deep-frying, and fry the pieces until they are golden brown and crisp. Drain on kitchen paper before eating.

sticky or glutinous rice *(khao niew)*

This is a broad short-grain rice, mostly white, although it can be brown, or even black. It is the staple of northern Thailand, where during the meal it is plucked with the fingers, rolled into a ball and used to scoop up the other food. It is also used throughout Thailand to make sweets. Sticky rice cannot be cooked in a rice cooker, and needs to be soaked before cooking.

Serves 4

450g sticky rice

1 Put the rice in a pan, cover with water and soak for at least 3 hours, or overnight if possible. Drain and rinse thoroughly.

2 Line the perforated part of a steamer with a double thickness of muslin or cheesecloth and turn the rice into it. Heat the water in the bottom of the steamer to boiling and steam the rice over a moderate heat for 30 minutes.

vegetarian fried rice *(khao pad mang sa virad)*

This is a vegetarian dish that is best cooked using whatever local seasonal vegetables are available, trying, if possible to create an interesting mix of vegetable textures and colours.

Serves 4

2 tablespoons oil
2 garlic cloves, finely chopped
6 tablespoons mixed cooked
   beans, e.g. mangetout and
   runner beans
2 tablespoons diced carrots
2 tablespoons diced tomato
2 tablespoons diced pineapple
2 tablespoons light soy sauce
1 teaspoon sugar
½ teaspoon ground white
   pepper
225g boiled fragrant rice (see
   page 176)
coriander leaves, to garnish

1 In a wok or frying pan, heat the oil and fry the garlic until golden brown. Stirring constantly, add each of the remaining ingredients in succession (except for the coriander).

2 Stir thoroughly, until the rice is heated through, then turn on to a serving dish and garnish with the coriander leaves.

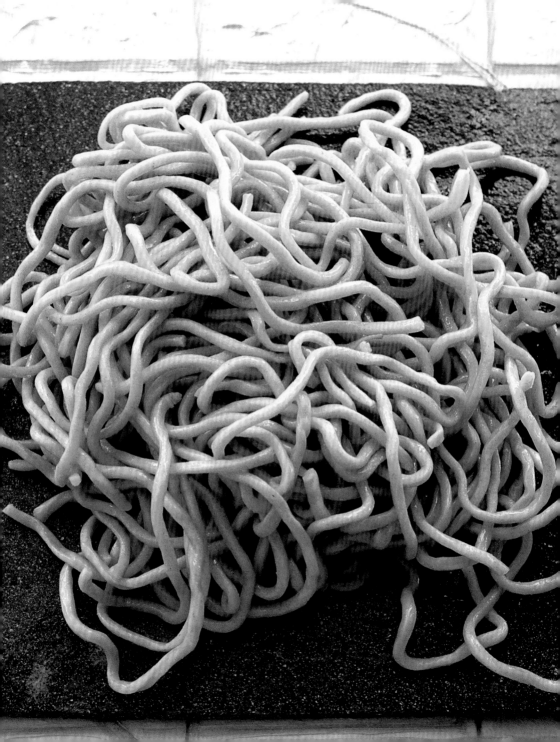

noodles *(gueyteow)*

Noodles are a Chinese invention, but have become the basic fast food of most of Asia. In Thailand there are noodle sellers everywhere, at more or less any time of the day or night.

Noodles are made from either rice flour or soya bean flour and there are six main varieties.

Sen yai
Sometimes called rice river noodle or rice stick, this is a broad, flat, white rice flour noodle. If bought fresh, the strands need to be separated before cooking.

Sen mee
A small, wiry noodle, sometimes called rice vermicelli.

Sen lek
A medium-sized, flat rice flour noodle. The city of Chantaburi is famous for these noodles, which are sometimes called Jantaboon noodles, after the nickname for the town.

Ba mee
An egg and rice flour noodle, yellow in colour, this comes in a variety of shapes, each with its own name. However, it is unlikely that you will see anything other than the commonest form, which is like a thin spaghetti, curled up in nests, which need to be shaken loose before cooking.

Wun sen
A very thin, wiry, translucent soya bean flour noodle, also called vermicelli or cellophane noodle.

Kanom jin
The one uniquely Thai noodle, made from rice flour mixed with water, then squeezed through a special sieve to make thick strands, like spaghetti. It is made only in large quantities for special occasions, usually temple festivals. Luckily there is a very similar Japanese noodle, *longxu*, which is sold dried in packets, in specialist shops.

cooking noodles

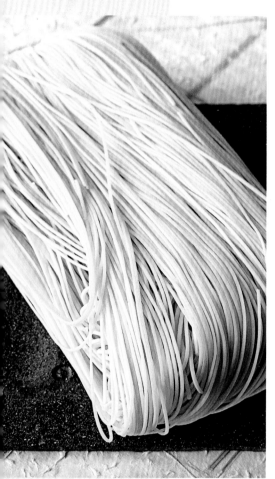

Fresh noodles can be cooked directly, whereas dried ones need to be soaked in water for a short while and rinsed before cooking. Follow the instructions on the packet. Noodles are often cooked twice: first they are blanched, then they are fried.

Noodle soups

The noodles are blanched in boiling water, then cooked with meat, fish and/or vegetables and served in a tasty stock (see page 185).

Dry noodles

Again the noodles are blanched in boiling water and cooked with the other ingredients, but this time they are mixed with a sauce before serving.

Deep-fried noodles

The noodles are deep-fried, then they are either mixed with a sauce or a sauce is poured on top.

Stir-fried noodles

The noodles are stir-fried in a wok with meat and vegetables.

stock recipes

meat stock

Remember, if you keep the stock, you must boil it every day, or pour it into containers and freeze it.

Simply cover the bones or carcasses with water, bring to the boil and simmer for 2 hours, skimming any foam off the surface from time to time, and adding water as necessary to cover the bones. Add no herbs or spices; these will be added according to each individual recipe.

500–750g bones
1.5 litres water

japanese stock *(dashi)*

1 Bring the water to the boil. Rinse the seaweed under cold water and add to the boiling water, stirring continuously for 3 minutes.

2 Remove the seaweed from the water, then add the shredded bonito. Bring back to the boil, stirring continuously, then remove the pan from the heat and leave it to stand for 5 minutes. Strain the liquid to remove the bones.

1.5 litres water
1 sheet (approximately 15 x 20cm) dried seaweed (kombu)
3 tablespoons shredded dried bonito (katsuobushi)

vegetable stock

Other vegetables may be substituted if desired, but avoid highly flavoured or coloured ones, such as beetroot. Do not add any other herbs or spices.

Cover the vegetables, coriander and peppercorns with the water, bring to the boil and simmer for 1 hour.

1 medium onion, peeled and halved
2 carrots, roughly cut
2 celery sticks, roughly cut
4 coriander stems
1 teaspoon whole black peppercorns
1.5 litres water

index

index

index

index

index